BIGGEST
FASTEST
DEADLIEST

THE BOOK OF FASCINATING FACTS

DAN BRIDGES

summersdale

BIGGEST, FASTEST, DEADLIEST

Summersdale Publishers Ltd
46 West Street
Chichester
West Sussex
PO19 1RP
UK

www.summersdale.com

Printed and bound in Great Britain

ISBN: 978-1-84953-084-2

Substantial discounts on bulk quantities of Summersdale books are available to corporations, professional associations and other organisations. For details contact Summersdale Publishers by telephone: +44 (0) 1243 771107, fax: +44 (0) 1243 786300 or email: nicky@summersdale.com.

CONTENTS

ANIMALS

THE WORLD'S LARGEST EVER...

RODENT	Capybara	South America	65 kg/1.3 m
LAND MAMMAL	Andrewsarchus*	Mongolia	180-450 kg/3.7 m
SEA MAMMAL	Blue Whale		80 t/33 m
MARSUPIAL	Diprotodon*	Australia	2.7 t/3 m
INSECT	Meganeura*	Europe	75 cm (wingspan)

* Now extinct.

TOP TEN WORLD'S BIGGEST ANIMALS ON LAND

1	African Elephant	8.5 t/6.66 m (21.85 ft)
2	Asian Elephant	4.2 t/5.94 m (19.5 ft)
3	White Rhinoceros	2.3 t/3.78 m (12.5 ft)
4	Hippopotamus	2.5 t/3.35 m (11 ft)
5	Gaur	1.6 t/2.99 m (9.8 ft)
6	Giraffe	1.4 t/4.69 m (15.4 ft)
7	Walrus	1.2 t/3.35 m (11 ft)
8	Black Rhinoceros	1.2 t/3.43 m (11.25 ft)
9	Saltwater Crocodile	785 kg/6.10 m (20 ft)
10	Wild Asian Water Buffalo	770 kg/3.47 m (11.4 ft)

TOP TEN WORLD'S FASTEST ANIMALS ON LAND

1	Cheetah	71 mph (114 km/h)
2	Pronghorn Antelope	57 mph (95 km/h)
3	Blue Wildebeest	50 mph (80 km/h)
4	Lion	50 mph (80 km/h)
5	Springbok	50 mph (80 km/h)
6	Brown Hare	48 mph (77 km/h)
7	Red Fox	48 mph (77 km/h)
8	Grant's Gazelle	47 mph (76 km/h)
9	Thomson's Gazelle	47 mph (76 km/h)
10	Horse	45 mph (72 km/h)

TOP TEN WORLD'S FASTEST ANIMALS IN WATER

1	Sailfish	70 mph (113 km/h)
2	Mako Shark	60 mph (97 km/h)
3	Marlin	50 mph (80 km/h)
4	Killer Whale	48 mph (77 km/h)
5	Wahoo	48 mph (77 km/h)
6	Tunny	46 mph (74 km/h)
7	Bluefish Tuna	44 mph (70 km/h)
8	Great Blue Shark	43 mph (69 km/h)
9	Bonefish	40 mph (64 km/h)
	Swordfish	40 mph (64 km/h)
10	Four-winged Flying Fish	35 mph (56 km/h)
	Tarpon	35 mph (56 km/h)

TOP TEN WORLD'S FASTEST ANIMALS IN THE AIR

1	Peregrine Falcon	200 mph (322 km/h)*
2	Spine-tailed Swift, aka the White-throated Needletail	106 mph (171 km/h)
3	Frigate Bird	95 mph (153 km/h)
4	Spur-winged Goose	88 mph (142 km/h)
5	Red-breasted Merganser	80 mph (129 km/h)
6	White-rumped Swift	77 mph (124 km/h)
7	Canvasback Duck	72 mph (116 km/h)
8	Eider Duck	70 mph (113 km/h)
9	Teal	68 mph (109 km/h)
10	Mallard	65 mph (105 km/h)

* This speed is achieved only through diving.

TOP TEN WORLD'S BIGGEST BIRDS (WINGSPANS)

1	Albatross	3.6 m (11.8 ft)
2	Eastern White Pelican	3.6 m (11.8 ft)
3	Andean Condor	3.2 m (10.5 ft)
4	Whooping Swan	2.99 m (9.8 ft)
5	Bearded Vulture	2.99 m (9.8 ft)
6	Turkey Vulture	2.8 m (9.2 ft)
7	Grey Crane	2.5 m (8.2 ft)
8	Golden Eagle	2.5 m (8.2 ft)
9	White Stork	1.8 m (5.9 ft)
10	Grey Heron	1.71 m (5.6 ft)

FASCINATING FACTS

- Peregrine falcons are the fastest animals in the world. They fly at an average of 90 mph (145 km/h).
- An elephant, despite its ponderous appearance, can reach speeds of up to 25 mph (40 km/h) on an open stretch.
- Sloths move so slowly that algae is formed on their coats, this is advantageous as it serves as camouflage and provides nutrients for the sloth when licked.

 COLLECTIVE NOUNS

Apes	Shrewdness	Larks	Exultation
Baboons	Congress	Leopards	Leap
Bears	Sleuth	Mice	Mischief
Butterflies	Rabble	Owls	Parliament
Cobras	Quiver	Penguins	Huddle
Doves	Piteousness	Rattlesnakes	Rhumba
Eagles	Convocation	Ravens	Unkindness
Emus	Mob	Rhinoceroses	Crash
Ferrets	Business	Rooks	Storytelling
Hawks	Kettle	Starlings	Murmuration
Lapwings	Deceit	Weasels	Sneak

TOP TEN WORLD'S DEADLIEST ANIMALS TO HUMANS

1   Mosquito
2   Asian Cobra
3   Australian Box Jellyfish
4   Great White Shark
5   African Lion
6   Australian Saltwater Crocodile
7   Elephant
8   Polar Bear
9   Cape Buffalo
10 Poison Dart Frog

FASCINATING FACTS

- A cockroach can survive without its head; entomologist Christopher Tipping decapitated cockroaches under a microscope and a couple lasted for several weeks in a jar.

- Many birds migrate, but the Arctic tern travels furthest. It flies from the Arctic to the Antarctic, and back again – a round trip of 32,000 kilometres.

- The iguana can survive in exceptionally high temperatures. Conversely, a thick layer of blubber provides polar bears with such excellent insulation that their body temperature and metabolic rate remain the same, even at –37°C.

ANIMALS' ABODES

Animal	Abode		Animal	Abode	
Badger	Sett	Earth	Lion	Den	Lair
Bear	Lair	Den	Mole	Fortress	
Beaver	Lodge		Otter	Holt	
Bee	Hive		Rabbit	Burrow	Warren
Bird	Nest		Squirrel	Drey	
Eagle	Eyrie		Tiger	Lair	
Fox	Earth	Lair	Wasp	Nest	Vespiary
Hare	Form				

TOP TEN WORLD'S LARGEST SPIDERS (AVERAGE LEG SPAN)

1	Huntsman Spider	300 mm
2	Brazilian Salmon Pink	270 mm
3	Brazilian Giant Tawny Red	260 mm
4	Goliath Tarantula	254 mm
5	Wolf Spider	254 mm
6	Purple Bloom Bird-eating Spider	230 mm
7	Colombian Lesser Black Tarantula	230 mm
8	Hercules Baboon Spider	203 mm
9	Hysterocrates Spider	178 mm
10	Cardinal Spider	140 mm

MAJOR EXTINCTIONS IN THE LAST 2,000 YEARS

MAMMAL	HABITAT	EXTINCTION
Auroch	Poland	1610
Caspian Tiger	South-west Russia	1960s
Caucasian Moose	Caucasus Mountains	1810
Caucasian Wisent	Caucasus Mountains	1927
Corsican Pika	Corsica	1800
Cyprus Spiny Mouse	Cyprus	1980
European Ass (Equus)	Spain	1400
European Lion	Greece	100
Majorcan Hare	Majorca	1980
Portuguese Ibex	Portugal	1892
Pyrenean Ibex	Spain	2000
Sardinian Pika	Sardinia	1800
Tarpan	Poland	1800

BIRD	HABITAT	EXTINCTION
Dodo	Mauritius	1600s
Great Auk	Iceland	1844
Cyprus Dipper	Cyprus	1950

REPTILE	HABITAT	EXTINCTION
Ratas Island Lizard	Menorca	1950
Santo Stefano Lizard	Santo Stefano Island	1965

TOP TEN WORLD'S MOST VENOMOUS ANIMALS

1	Box Jellyfish
2	King Cobra
3	Marbled Cone Snail
4	Blue-ringed Octopus
5	Death Stalker Scorpion
6	Stonefish
7	The Brazilian Wandering Spider
8	Inland Taipan
9	Poison Dart Frog
10	Puffer Fish

FASCINATING FACTS

- There have been 5,567 recorded deaths caused by box jellyfish since 1954. They have up to 60 tentacles and each one contains enough toxin to kill 50 people.
- The inland taipan carries enough venom to kill 100 people, but there are no recorded fatalities.
- A bite from a funnel-web spider can kill a person in 15 minutes.

TOP TEN WORLD'S MOST ENDANGERED SPECIES IN 2010

1	Tiger	3,200
2	Polar Bear	20-25,000
3	Pacific Walrus	less than 200,000
4	Magellanic Penguin	less than 200,000 pairs
5	Leatherback Turtle	2,300 recorded adult females
6	Bluefin Tuna	unknown*
7	Mountain Gorilla	680
8	Monarch Butterfly	unknown**
9	Javan Rhinoceros	less than 60
10	Giant Panda	1,600

* Although no fixed figure is available, it is believed that the biomass of the adult population has decreased by 90 per cent in recent years.
** The yearly migration of this butterfly, taking shelter in eucalyptus, pine, and cypress trees is severely under threat from illegal logging.

TOP TEN WORLD'S BIGGEST DINOSAURS

1	Argentinosaurus	100 t/36.58 m (120 ft)
2	Sauroposeidon	over 60 t/29.87 m (98 ft)
3	Spinosaurus	13 t/15.85 m (52 ft)
4	Liopleurodon	30 t/15.24 m (50 ft)
5	Shonisaurus	30 t/15.24 m (50 ft)
6	Shantungosaurus	50 t/15.24 m (50 ft)
7	Quetzalcoatlus	100 kg/13.72 m (45 ft)
8	Sarcosuchus	8 t/12.19 m (40 ft)
9	Utahraptor	0.68 t/6.10 m (20 ft)
10	Moschops	1 t/4.88 m (16 ft)

- The first fossil ever investigated was the femur of a megalosaurus found in 1676 in England. When the fragment was discovered, one Oxford professor concluded that it belonged to a giant human!
- The fossilised remains of an archaeopteryx were discovered in 1860–62 in Solnhofen, Germany. They were found around the time that Charles Darwin's *The Origin of Species* was first published and this fossil confirmed an evolutionary link between dinosaurs and birds.

TOP TEN WORLD'S SMALLEST ANIMALS (LENGTH)

1	Fairy Fly	0.24 mm
2	Anglerfish	7.9 mm
3	Paedocypris Fish	7.9 mm
4	Brazilian Gold Frog	9.8 mm
5	Jaragua Sphaero or Dwarf Gecko Lizard	15.24 mm
6	Seahorse	16 mm
7	Mr Peewee (smallest hamster)	22.86 mm
8	Brookesia Minima Chameleon	38.1 mm
9	Bee Hummingbird	57.15 mm
10	Thread snake	100 mm

- Weighing less than an ounce, Mr Peewee, the smallest hamster in the world, is only just bigger than a fifty pence piece and can fit inside a matchbox.
- The world's smallest recorded insects are feather-winged beetles and parasitic wasps found in the New World tropics. The smallest ones are 0.21 mm long and they outwardly show the features of an insect whilst having the full complement of internal organs.

 ## TOP TEN WORLD'S BIGGEST FISH

1	Whale Shark	11.8 t*/12.65 m (41.5 ft)
2	Basking Shark	5.2 t/12.27 m (40.3 ft)
3	Great White Shark	2.3 t/6 m (19.7 ft)
4	Ocean Sunfish	1 t/3.2 m (10.5 ft)
5	Giant Cambodian Stingray	455 kg/5.03 m (16.5 ft)
6	Pirarucu	180 kg/3.05 m (16.5 ft)
7	Mekong Giant Catfish	293 kg/2.7 m (8.9 ft)
8	Beluga or European Sturgeon	264 kg/8.6 m (28.2 ft)
9	Bull Shark	318 kg/4 m (13.1 ft)
10	Wels Catfish	150 kg/3 m (9.8 m)

* The heaviest whale shark ever found weighed 36 tons.

TOP TEN WORLD'S SMELLIEST ANIMALS

1	Zorilla
2	Skunk
3	Porcupine
4	Tasmanian Devil
5	Ferret
6	Turkey Vulture
7	Kakapo
8	Mink Frog
9	Stinkpot Turtle
10	Darkling Beetle

FASCINATING FACTS

- The zorilla, or striped polecat, lives in arid regions of southern Africa. Its smell is so potent that it can tickle your nostril hairs from half a mile away!

- Herrings communicate through farting. And they fart all the time, which means they must have a lot to talk about!

- The elusive, sweet-toothed binturong is a member of the civet family, and lives in the tropical forests of southern Asia. It's a bizarre animal with a scent that is said to smell like buttered popcorn.

- Termites, not cows, are the undisputed fart champions of the world. It is estimated they are responsible for as much as 11 per cent of all global methane emissions – twice as much as cows.

TOP TEN WORLD'S LONGEST-LIVING ANIMALS

1	Quahog (marine clam)	200 years
2	Giant Tortoise	150 years
3	Greek Tortoise	110 years
4	Killer Whale	90 years
5	European Eel	88 years
6	Lake Sturgeon	82 years
7	Sea Anemone	80 years
8	Elephant	78 years
9	Freshwater Mussel	75 years
10	Whale Shark	70 years

TOP TEN LONGEST GESTATION PERIODS

1	Shark (Basking, Frilled, Spiny Dogfish)	730-1,095 days
2	Black Alpine Salamander	730+ days
3	African Elephant	660 days
4	Asiatic Elephant	600 days
5	Baird's Beaked Whale	520 days
6	White Rhinoceros	490 days
7	Walrus	480 days
8	Giraffe	460 days
9	Velvet Worm	455 days
10	Tapir	400 days

ART AND
ARTISTS

# NATURAL PIGMENTS

Crimson (red)	insect called *Kermes vermilio*
Ultramarine (blue)	lapis lazuli
Indigo (dark purple)	extract of indigofera plant or the woad or glastum plant
Tyrian Purple (reddy purple)	secretions of the sea snail
Cochineal (red)	the cochineal insect
Burnt Sienna (brown)	iron oxide
Verdigris (green)	copper and vinegar mix

THE FIVE MAJOR ORDERS OF CLASSICAL ARCHITECTURE

1. Doric – fluted shafts; three vertical bands and square panels
2. Ionic – densely fluted shafts, scrolls carved on capital
3. Corinthian – fluted column and capital, carved with two rows of four acanthus leaves and scrolls
4. Tuscan – Roman adaptation of Doric; plain shaft, no fluting
5. Composite – Roman blend of Ionic scrolls and Corinthian acanthus leaves

TOP FIVE WORLD'S MOST PROLIFIC ARTISTS

1 Morris Katz (1932-present) - over 280,000 works (and counting)
2 Pablo Picasso (1881-1973) - 147,800 works
3 Ik-Joong Kang (1960-present) - 40,000 paintings
4 Pierre-Auguste Renoir (1841-1919) - 6,000 paintings
5 Bahruz Kangarli (1892-1922) - nearly 4,000 works

TOP TEN WORLD'S MOST EXPENSIVE PAINTINGS EVER SOLD

1 *Number 5, 1948*, Jackson Pollock: $140 million (private sale 2006)
2 *Woman III*, Willem De Kooning: $137.5 million (private sale 2006)
3 *Portrait of Adele Bloch-Bauer*, Gustav Klimt: $135 million (private sale 2006)
4 *Nu au Plateau de Sculpteur*, Pablo Picasso: $106.5 million (Christie's 2010)
5 *Garçon à la Pipe*, Pablo Picasso: $104.1 million (Sotheby's 2004)
6 *Eight Elvises*, Andy Warhol: $100 million (private sale 2008)
7 *Dora Maar au Chat*, Pablo Picasso: $95.2 million (Sotheby's 2006)
8 *Triptych 1976*, Francis Bacon: $86.3 million (Sotheby's 2008)
9 *Portrait of Doctor Gachet*, Vincent Van Gogh: $82.5 million (Christie's 1990)
10 *Le Bassin Aux Nymphéas*, Claude Monet: $80,451,178 (Christie's 2008)

TOP FIVE WORLD'S MOST VALUABLE ART THEFTS

1   Isabella Stewart Gardner Museum, Boston, 1990 – 13 paintings: over $500 million

2   Van Gogh Museum, Amsterdam, 1991 – 20 paintings: $500 million

3   National Gallery, London, 1961 – *Duke of Wellington* by Goya: $400,000*

4   E. G. Buehrle Collection, Zurich, 2008 – four major works: $163 million

5   Marmottan Museum, Paris, 1985 – nine paintings: $12.5 million

* Value at the time of the robbery.

FASCINATING FACTS

- When three ski-masked men snatched a Cézanne, a Degas, a Van Gogh and a Monet (together worth an estimated $163 million) from a Zurich museum, they failed to take the most expensive paintings in the collection.

- Benvenuto Cellini's *Saliera*, known as the '*Mona Lisa* of sculpture' and worth $60 million, spent two years under the bed of the first-time thief before any attempt was made to ransom it.

- While revellers partied during the 2006 carnival, four armed men used the chaos to make off with paintings worth at least $20 million from a Rio de Janeiro museum.

- Goya's famous painting of the Duke of Wellington was snatched from London's National Gallery in 1961 only to reappear in the lair of Doctor No during the first James Bond film. The real painting was returned voluntarily six years later.

TOP TEN WORLD'S MOST FAKED ARTISTS

1 Giorgio de Chirico (1888-1978)
2 Jean-Baptiste-Camille Corot (1796-1875)
3 Salvador Dalí (1904-89)
4 Honoré Daumier (1808-79)
5 Vincent Van Gogh (1853-90)
6 Kazimir Malevich (1878-1935)
7 Amedeo Modigliani (1884-1920)
8 Frederic Remington (1861-1909)
9 Auguste Rodin (1840-1917)
10 Maurice Utrillo (1883-1955)

TOP TEN WORLD'S BIGGEST ARTWORKS

1 *Mundi Man* or *Eldee Man*, Ando: 4 million sq m (43.06 million sq ft)
2 *Surrounded Islands*, Christo: 603,850 sq m (6.5 million sq ft)
3 *The Wave*, Djuro Siroglavic: 13,000 sq m (139,932 sq ft)
4 *Mother Earth*, David Aberg: 7,989 sq m (86,000 sq ft)
5 *Smiley Face*, Robb College students, Australia: 6,729 sq m (72,437 sq ft)
6 *Hero*, Eric Waugh: 3,846 sq m (41,400 sq ft)
7 *Borodino Panorama*, Franz Roubaud: 1,725 sq m (18,567 sq ft)
8 *The Big Picture*, Ando: 1,200 sq m (12,916 sq ft)
9 *Panorama Mesdag*, Hendrik Willem Mesdag: 1,145.9 sq m (12,334 sq ft)
10 *The Battle of Atlanta*, American Panorama Company: 947.43 sq m (10,198 sq ft)

- Large-scale artist Ando, 'painted' onto the landscape of the Mundi Mundi Plains in New South Wales, Australia, creating an artwork more than six times larger than the previous 'largest work of art in the world' completed by Christo when he wrapped 11 islands in Florida, USA.

TURNER PRIZE WINNERS
(1999–2009)

YEAR	ARTIST
1999	Steve McQueen
2000	Wolfgang Tillmans
2001	Martin Creed
2002	Keith Tyson
2003	Grayson Perry
2004	Jeremy Deller
2005	Simon Starling
2006	Tomma Abts
2007	Mark Wallinger
2008	Mark Leckey
2009	Richard Wright

- Damien Hirst is known for his controversial artworks, none more so than his *Mother and Child Divided*, which showed a cow and a calf cut into sections and exhibited in a series of separate vitrines.

- Tracey Emin's infamous installation *Everyone I Have Ever Slept With 1963-1995* consisted of a tent which had the 102 names of her past lovers sewn into the lining. It was destroyed in a warehouse fire in 2004.

TOP FIVE MOST VALUABLE ARTWORKS BY DAMIEN HIRST*

1. *For the Love of God* (diamond-encrusted human skull) £50 million
2. *The Golden Calf* (bullock in formaldehyde) £10.3 million
3. *The Kingdom* (tiger shark in formaldehyde) £9.6 million
4. *The Physical Impossibility of Death in the Mind of Someone Living* (14 ft tiger shark immersed in formaldehyde in a vitrine) £6.5 million
5. *Fragments of Paradise* (stainless steel, glass and diamonds) £5.2 million

* Figures show amount that each artwork realised when sold.

TOP TEN WORLD'S OLDEST ARTWORKS

1 Auditorium Cave Petroglyphs (rock carvings), Madhya Pradesh, Central India: 290,000-700,000 BC

2 Daraki-Chattan Cave Petroglyphs (rock carvings), Madhya Pradesh, Central India: 290,000-700,000 BC

3 Venus of Berekhat Ram (basaltic figurine), Golan Heights, Israel: 230,000-700,000 BC

4 Venus of Tan-Tan (quartzite figurine), Tan-Tan, Morocco: 200,000-500,000 BC

5 Blombos Cave Rock Art, South Africa: 70,000 BC

6 La Ferrassie Cave Cupules (cupules on a Neanderthal tomb), Les Eyzies, Dordogne, France: 70,000-40,000 BC

7 Swabian Jura Ivory Carvings, Germany: 33,000-30,000 BC

8 Bone Venus of Kostenky, Russia: 30,000 BC

9 Venus of Monpazier (steatite statuette), France: 30,000 BC

10 Chauvet Cave Paintings, Ardeche, France: 30,000-23,000 BC

FASCINATING FACTS

- Visitors to the State Hermitage Museum in St Petersburg, Russia have to walk 15 miles to see the 322 galleries, housing nearly three million works of art.

- As an engineer, Leonardo da Vinci conceived ideas vastly ahead of his own time, conceptually inventing a helicopter, a tank, the use of concentrated solar power, a calculator, a rudimentary theory of plate tectonics, the double hull and many others.

- In 1961, Matisse's *Le Bateau* (*The Boat*) hung upside down for two months in the Museum of Modern Art, New York (none of the 116,000 visitors had noticed).

- Vincent Van Gogh sold only one painting in his entire life. It was to his brother who owned an art gallery. The painting was *Red Vineyards at Arles*.

COMPUTER SCIENCE

KEY DATES IN THE
HISTORY OF COMPUTERS

1833 Charles Babbage designed the first general purpose 'Analytical Engine'.

1842 Ada Augusta King, Countess of Lovelace, weaved instructions on punched cards, based on a language compatible with the 'Analytical Engine' – the first computer program.

1941 Konrad Zuse developed his Z-3 computer in Berlin, Germany, which used the binary number system and performed floating-point arithmetic.

1946 Konrad Zuse developed the world's first programming language: Plankalk.

1949 Maurice Wilkes and the staff of the Mathematical Laboratory at Cambridge University developed EDSAC, the first fully functional stored-program electronic digital computer.

1950 The floppy disk was invented at the Imperial University in Tokyo by Doctor Yoshiro Nakamats.

1976 The first Apple computer – the Apple 1 – is shown to the public.

1990 Tim Berners-Lee invents the World Wide Web in 1990.

TOP TEN WORLD'S FASTEST SUPERCOMPUTERS AND THEIR MANUFACTURERS*

	COMPUTER	YEAR OF RELEASE	COMPANY
1	Jaguar Cray XT5-HE Opteron 6 Core	2009	Cray Inc.
2	Nebulae Dawning TC3600 Blade	2010	Dawning
3	Roadrunner Bladecenter QS22/LS21 Cluster	2009	IBM
4	Kraken XT5 Cray XT5-HE Opteron 6 Core	2009	Cray Inc.
5	JUGENE Blue Gene/P Solution	2010	IBM
6	Pleiades SGI Altix ICE	2010	SGI
7	Tianhe-1 NUDT TH-1 Cluster	2009	NUDT
8	BlueGene/L eServer Blue Gene Solution	2007	IBM
9	Intrepid Blue Gene/P Solution	2007	IBM
10	Red Sky Sun Blade x6275	2010	Sun Microsystems

* Information compiled in June 2010.

UNITS OF DATA

1 Bit: The smallest unit of data used by a computer
4 Bits: Nybble (Semioctet)
8 Bits: Byte (Octet) (a character of information e.g. 'a')
16 Bits: Word (two Octets)
32 Bits: Dword
64 Bits: Qword
1 Kilobyte: A thousand characters of information
1 Megabyte: A million characters of information
1 Gigabyte: A billion characters of information
1 Terabyte: A thousand billion characters of information

TOP TEN WORLD'S BEST-SELLING VIDEO GAME CONSOLES

	CONSOLE	YEAR OF RELEASE	UNITS SOLD
1	Sony PlayStation 2	2000	142.8 million
2	Sony PlayStation	1994	102.49 million
3	Nintendo Wii	2006	70.93 million
4	Nintendo Entertainment System	1983	61.91 million
5	Super Nintendo Entertainment System	1990	49.1 million
6	Microsoft Xbox 360	2005	39 million
7	Sega Mega Drive/Genesis	1988	38.7 million
8	Sony PlayStation 3	2006	35.7 million
9	Nintendo 64	1996	32.93 million
10	Atari 2600	1977	30 million

FASCINATING FACTS

- The commercial for the Macintosh – Apple's first Apple Mac computer – was made by *Alien* director Ridley Scott and cost $1.5 million.
- Over 260 million iPods have been sold worldwide as of April 2010.
- Approximately 1.7 million iPhone 4 models were sold in its first month of release in June 2010.

PRODUCT	YEAR OF RELEASE	DESCRIPTION
Apple I	1976	personal computer
Apple II	1977	personal computer
Apple III	1980	personal computer
Lisa	1983	personal computer
Macintosh 128K	1984	first original Apple Mac
Macintosh Portable	1989	Apple's first battery-powered portable PC
Powerbook	1991	laptop
Power Macintosh	1994	workstation PC
IMac	1998	desktop PC
IBook	1999	laptop
IPod	2001	portable media player
Mac Mini	2005	small form factor laptop/server
MacBook	2006	laptop*
Apple TV	2007	digital media receiver
IPhone	2007	slate smartphone
Macbook Air	2008	ultraportable laptop
IPad	2010	tablet media player/PC

* The best-selling Macintosh in history.

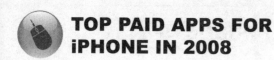

TOP PAID APPS FOR iPHONE IN 2008

1	*Koi Pond*
2	*Texas Hold'em*
3	*Moto Chaser*
4	*Crash Bandicoot: Nitro Kart 3D*
5	*Super Monkey Ball*
6	*Cro-Mag Rally*
7	*Enigmo*
8	*Pocket Guitar*
9	*Recorder*
10	*iBeer*

TOP TEN MOST POPULAR WEBSITES ON THE INTERNET*

1	Google.com
2	Yahoo.com
3	Youtube.com
4	Live.com
5	Facebook.com
6	Msn.com
7	Wikipedia.org
8	Blogger.com
9	Myspace.com
10	Yahoo.co.jp

* List compiled in June 2010.

TOP TEN MOST DOWNLOADED MICROSOFT SOFTWARE

1	Microsoft Office Compatibility Pack for Word, Excel, and PowerPoint File Formats
2	DirectX End-User Runtime
3	Update for Windows XP (KB932823)
4	.NET Framework Version 2.0 Redistributable Package (x86)
5	Microsoft .NET Framework 4 (Web Installer)
6	Windows 7 Upgrade Advisor
7	.NET Framework 3.5
8	Windows Internet Explorer 7 for Windows XP
9	Windows Media Components for QuickTime
10	.NET Framework 3.5 Service pack 1

MOST POPULAR SEARCH ENGINES IN THE USA*

SEARCH ENGINE	VOLUME OF VISITORS
Google	71.65 per cent
Yahoo	14.37 per cent
Bing	9.85 per cent
Ask	2.19 per cent
AOL	1.15 per cent
Other	0.79 per cent

* List compiled in June 2010.

- Bill Gates earns approximately $243 a second. If Bill Gates was a country, he would be the thirty-seventh richest country on earth.

TOP TEN MOST POPULAR
SEARCHES ON GOOGLE*

1	michael jackson
2	facebook
3	tuenti
4	twitter
5	sanalika
6	new moon
7	lady gaga
8	windows 7
9	dantri.com.vn
10	torpedo gratis

* Ranked in order of the queries with the largest volume of searches in June 2010.

TOP TEN DEADLIEST COMPUTER VIRUSES

1	The Morris Worm – affected ten per cent of all computers connected to the Internet in November 1998
2	The Concept Virus – infects Microsoft Word documents
3	CIH aka The Chernobyl Virus – overwrites a chip, paralysing the computer
4	The Anna Kournikova Worm – attachment posing as a photo of the tennis player
5	ILOVEYOU aka The Love Bug – designed to steal Internet access passwords
6	The Melissa Virus – mass-mailing macro virus, inserted a *Simpsons* quote into Word documents
7	The Blaster Worm – launched a denial of service attack against Microsoft's website
8	Sasser Computer Worm – over a million computers infected
9	Solar Sunrise – took control of over 500 systems belonging to the army, government and private sector in the USA in February 1998
10	Code Red Worm – developed in July 2001 to use the power of all infected computers against the White House website, estimated damage $2 billion

ENGINEERING
AND
INVENTIONS

TOP TEN WORLD'S LONGEST SUSPENSION BRIDGES

1	Akashi-Kaikyo Bridge	Japan	1,991 m (6,532 ft)
2	The Great Belt Bridge (Storebæltsbroen)	Denmark	1,624 m (5,328 ft)
3	Runyang Bridge	China	1,490 m (4,888 ft)
4	Humber Bridge	England	1,410 m (4,626 ft)
5	Jiangyin Bridge	China	1,385 m (4,543 ft)
6	Tsing Ma Bridge	China	1,377 m (4,518 ft)
7	Verrazano-Narrows Bridge	USA	1,298 m (4,260 ft)
8	Golden Gate Bridge	USA	1,280 m (4,200 ft)
9	High Coast Bridge (Högakustenbron)	Sweden	1,210 m (3,970 ft)
10	Mackinac Bridge	USA	1,158 m (3,800 ft)

TOP TEN WORLD'S LONGEST TUNNELS

1	Seikan Tunnel	Japan	33.5 miles (53.9 km)
2	Channel Tunnel	UK/France	31.3 miles (50.4 km)
3	Lötschberg Base Tunnel	Switzerland	21.5 miles (34.6 km)
4	Iwate-Ichinohe Tunnel	Japan	16 miles (25.7 km)
5	Lærdal Tunnel	Norway	15.2 miles (24.5 km)
6	Daishimizu Tunnel	Japan	13.8 miles (22.2 km)
7	Wushaoling Tunnel	China	13.1 miles (21.1 km)
8	Simplon Tunnel	Switzerland/Italy	12.3 miles (19.8 km)
9	Vereina Tunnel	Switzerland	11.8 miles (19 km)
10	Shin Kanmon Tunnel	Japan	11.6 miles (18.7 km)

TOP TEN WORLD'S
TALLEST BUILDINGS*

1	Burj Khalifa	Dubai, UAE	828 m (2,717 ft) 162 floors
2	Taipei 101	Taipei, Taiwan	509 m (1,670 ft) 101 floors
3	Shanghai World Financial Center	Shanghai, China	492 m (1,614 ft) 101 floors
4	Petronas Tower I and II	Kuala Lumpur, Malaysia	452 m (1,483 ft) 88 floors
5	Willis Tower	Chicago, USA	442 m (1,450 ft) 110 floors
6	Jin Mao Building	Shanghai, China	421 m 1,381 ft) 88 floors
7	Two International Finance Centre	Hong Kong, China	415 m (1,362 ft) 88 floors
8	CITIC Plaza	Guangzhou, China	391 m (1,283 ft) 80 floors
9	Shun Hing Square	Shenzhen, China	384 m (1,260 ft) 69 floors
10	Empire State Building	New York, USA	381 m (1,250 ft) 102 floors

* Ranking by highest architectural structural element, i.e. spires, statues etc. not antennae or flagpoles. For example the Malaysian Petronas Towers (with spire on top) is ranked higher than the Sears Tower, USA (with antenna on top) despite having a lower roof and a lower highest point (of spire/antenna).

TOP TEN WORLD'S LONGEST VEHICULAR BRIDGES

1	Lake Pontchartrain Causeway	USA	38,412 m (126,024 ft)
2	Manchac Swamp Bridge of I-55	USA	36,698m (120,400 ft)
3	Donghai Bridge	China	32,499 m (106,627 ft)
4	Atchafalaya Swamp Freeway Bridge of I-10	USA	29,289 m (96,095 ft)
5	No. 1 Bridge of Tianjin Binhai Mass Transit	China	25,799 m (84,645 ft)
6	Chesapeake Bay Bridge-Tunnel	USA	24,140 m (79,200 ft)
7	Bonnet Carré Spillway Bridge of I-10	USA	17,702 m (58,077 ft)
8	Vasco da Gama Bridge	Portugal	17,185 m (56,381 ft)
9	Penang Bridge	Malaysia	13,499 m (44,291 ft)
10	Kam Sheung Road-Tuen Mun Viaduct	Hong Kong	13,399 m (43,963 ft)

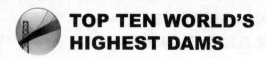

TOP TEN WORLD'S HIGHEST DAMS

1	Rogun	Tajikistan	335 m (1,098 ft)
2	Nurek	Tajikistan	300 m (984 ft)
3	Grande Dixence	Switzerland	285 m (935 ft)
4	Longtan	China	285 m (935 ft)
5	Inguri	Georgia	272 m (892 ft)
6	Borucu	Costa Rica	267 m (876 ft)
7	Vaiont	Italy	262 m (859 ft)
8	Manuel M. Torres	Mexico	261 m (856 ft)
9	Tehri	India	261 m (856 ft)
10	Eratan	China	245 m (804 ft)

FASCINATING FACTS

- One of the oldest man-made structures still standing is the Step Pyramid at Saqqara in Egypt. Built as a tomb for Pharaoh Djoser, it is believed to have been constructed between 2667 and 2648 BC.

- The Neolithic temple of Hagar Qim located on the Mediterranean island of Malta is thought to date back to the Ġgantija phase in 3600-3200 BC.

- The oldest known collective human settlement with buildings is Catal Huyuk and dates back to around 7800 BC.

- A structure thought to be the world's oldest building – twice the age of the pyramids – has been found beneath the sea off the coast of Japan and consists of a rectangular stone ziggurat believed to have been built in 8000 BC.

TOP TEN LONGEST BRITISH RAIL TUNNELS

1	Severn	Bristol to Newport	4.28 miles (6.88 km)
2	Totley	Manchester to Sheffield	3.44 miles (5.70 km)
3	Standedge	Manchester to Huddersfield	3.04 miles (4.89 km)
4	Sodbury	Swindon to Bristol	2.53 miles (4.06 km)
5	Strood	Medway, Kent	2.24 miles (3.61 km)
6	Disley	Stockport to Sheffield	2.2 miles (3.54 km)
7	Ffestiniog	Llandudno to Blaenau Ffestiniog	2.14 miles (3.44 km)
8	Bramhope	Horsforth to Weeton	2.14 miles (3.44 km)
9	Cowburn	Manchester to Sheffield	2.1 miles (3.39 km)
10	North Downs	Maidstone, Kent	1.99 miles (3.2 km)

FASCINATING FACTS

- There are some 10,460 miles (16,833 kilometres) of railway in the UK.
- The longest station platform in the UK is at Gloucester station and is 602.6 m (1,977 ft) long.
- British Rail has 40,000 bridges, tunnels and viaducts, as well as around 9,000 level crossings and over 1,100 signal boxes.

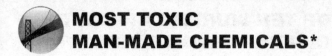

MOST TOXIC
MAN-MADE CHEMICALS*

1	Aldrin
2	Chlordane
3	DDT
4	Dieldrin
5	Endrin
6	Heptachlor
7	Mirex
8	Toxaphene
9	Polychlorinated biphenols (PCBs)
10	Hexachlorobenzene

* These chemicals are on a list produced for the 2001 Stockholm
Convention on Persistent Organic Pollutants (POPs).

TOP FIVE WORLD'S
BIGGEST MINES

1	Argyle (diamond mine)	Kimberley, Western Australia	450 sq km/600 m deep
2	Bingham (copper mine)	Utah, USA	4 km long/1.2 km deep
3	Escondida (copper mine)	Chile	3.2 km long / 749 m deep
4	Mirny (diamond mine)	Russia	1.2 km long/525 m deep
5	Udachnaya (diamond mine)	Sakha Republic, Russia	600 m deep

TOP TEN WORLD'S BIGGEST POWER STATIONS BY OUTPUT

1	Three Gorges Dam (hydroelectric)	China	22,500 MW
2	Itaipu Dam (hydroelectric)	Brazil/Paraguay	14,000 MW
3	Xiluodu Dam (hydroelectric)	China	12,600 MW
4	Guri Dam (hydroelectric)	Venezuela	10,200 MW
5	Tucurui Dam (hydroelectric)	Brazil	8,370 MW
6	Kashiwazaki-Kariwa Nuclear Power Plant	Japan	8,212 MW
7	Bruce Nuclear Generating Station	Canada	7,276 MW
8	Grand Coulee Dam (hydroelectric)	USA	6,809 MW
9	Sayano-Shushenskaya Dam (hydroelectric)	Russia	6,400 MW
	Xiangjiaba Dam (hydroelectric)	China	6,400 MW
10	Krasnoyarsk Hydroelectric Dam (hydroelectric)	Russia	6,000 MW

TOP TEN WORLD'S LARGEST DIAMONDS

1	Golden Jubilee	545.67 ct
2	Star of Africa	530.20 ct
3	Incomparable	407.48 ct
4	The Cullinan II Diamond	317.40 ct
5	Spirit of de Grisogono	312.24 ct
6	Centenary	273.83 ct
7	Jubilee	245.35 ct
8	The De Beers	234.65 ct
9	The Red Cross	205.07 ct
10	Millennium Star	203.40 ct

FASCINATING FACTS

- The depth of the Mirny diamond mine hole is such that wind currents inside cause a downdraft that has resulted in helicopters being sucked in. It produces 10 million cts of diamonds per year.
- The famous Hope diamond is supposedly cursed. Legend has it that the jewel was removed from the eye socket of a Hindu statue in India and has since brought bad luck to its subsequent owners in the form of bankruptcy, insanity, suicide and even being torn apart by wild dogs!

THE MOHS SCALE*

Talc
Gypsum
Calcite
Fluorite
Apatite
Orthoclase
Quartz
Topaz
Corundum
Diamond

* Named after German mineralogist Friedrich Mohs, the scale is used for comparing relative hardness of minerals. Each mineral on the scale can be scratched by the harder ones below it.

TOP FIVE WORLD'S LONGEST HIGHWAYS

1   Pan-American Highway, North Alaska to Argentina 30,000 miles (48,280 km)

2   Highway 1, Australia miles 15,534 miles (25,000 km)

3   Trans-Siberian Highway, St Petersburg to Vladivostok, Russia 6,835 miles (11,000 km)

4   Trans-Canada Highway, Vancouver Island to St John's, Newfoundland 4,860 miles (7,821 km)

5   Route 6, Provincetown, Massachusetts to Brewster, New York, USA 3,205 miles (5,158 km)

TOP TEN WORLD'S MOST DANGEROUS ROADS

1	North Yungas Road aka the 'Road of Death'	China
2	Sichuan-Tibet Highway	China
3	The Pan-American Highway	North Alaska to Argentina
4	Coastal Roads	Croatia
5	Guoliang Tunnel	Taihang Mountains, China
6	Halsema Highway	Philippines
7	Grimsel Pass	Switzerland
8	Taroko	Taiwan
9	Karakoram Highway	Pakistan to China
10	Skippers Canyon	New Zealand

FASCINATING FACTS

- The North Yungas is believed to be the most dangerous road in the world. It stretches for about forty mountain-hugging miles and is only 10 ft wide.

- 'Guoliang' translates from the Chinese as the 'road that does not tolerate any mistakes'. The road is 4.5 m high and 3.7 m wide with 30 windows to enjoy the dramatic landscape.

TOP TEN WORLD'S TALLEST CHURCHES

1	Sagrada Familia	Barcelona, Spain*	170 m (558 ft)
2	Ulm Cathedral	Ulm, Germany	162 m (530 ft)
3	Rouen Cathedral	Rouen, France	158 m (518 ft)
4	Cologne Cathedral	Cologne, Germany	157 m (516 ft)
5	Our Lady of Peace Basilica	Yamoussoukro, Ivory Coast	149 m (489 ft)
6	St Nicholas Church	Hamburg, Germany	147 m (482 ft)
7	Notre-Dame Cathedral	Strasbourg, France	144 m (472 ft)
8	Queen of Peace Shrine and Basilica	Lichen, Poland	140 m (459 ft)
9	Basilica of St Peter	Rome, Italy	138 m (452 ft)
10	St Stephen's Cathedral	Vienna, Austria	137 m (448 ft)

* To be completed in 2026.

INVENTIONS AND THEIR INVENTORS

INVENTION	INVENTOR	PLACE	YEAR
Adding Machine	Blaise Pascal	France	1642
Aeroplane	Orville and Wilbur Wright	USA	1903
Ambulance	Jean Dominique Larrey	France	1792
Aqualung	Jacques Cousteau and Emile Gagnan	France	1943
Atomic Bomb	Otto Frisch, Niels Bohr, Rudolf Peierls	Austria, Denmark, Germany	1939-45, 1939-45, 1939-45
Automatic Loom	Joseph-Marie Jacquard	France	1801
Ballpoint Pen	Ladislao Biro	Hungary	1944
Barometer	Evangelista Torricelli	Italy	1643
Battery (electric)	Alessandro Volta	Italy	1800
Bicycle (self-propelled)	Kirkpatrick MacMillan	UK	1839-40
Bouncing Bomb	Barnes Wallis	UK	1943
Car (internal combustion)	Gottlieb Daimler	Germany	1884
Car (petrol)	Karl Benz	Germany	1886
Cash Register	William Burroughs	USA	1892
Cat's Eyes	Percy Shaw	UK	1934
Cement (Portland)	Joseph Aspdin	UK	1824
Cinema	Auguste and Louis Lumière	France	1895

INVENTION	INVENTOR	PLACE	YEAR
Clock (mechanical)	Yi-Hsing	China	AD 725
Coffee (instant)	Nestlé	Switzerland	1937
Contraceptive Pill	Gregor Pincus	USA	1950
Credit Card	Ralph Scheider and Frank McNamara	USA	1950
Crossword	Arthur Wynne	USA	1913
Diesel Engine	Rudolf Diesel	Germany	1894
Electric Chair	H. Brown and E. Kenneally	USA	1888
Electric Guitar	Rickenbacker, Barth and Beauchamp	USA	1931
Electric Light Bulb	Thomas Alva Edison	USA	1879
Electric Telegraph	Georges Louis Lesage	Switzerland	1774
Escalator	Jesse W. Reno	USA	1892
Film (with soundtrack)	Lee de Forest	USA	1919
Flying Shuttle	John Kay	UK	1733
Fountain Pen	Lewis E. Waterman	USA	1884
Frozen Food Processor	Clarence Birdseye	USA	1929
Helicopter (first manned)	Louis and Jacques Breguet	France	1907
Hovercraft	Christopher Cockerell	UK	1956
Jeans	Levi-Strauss	USA	1872
Jet Engine	Frank Whittle	UK	1930

INVENTION	INVENTOR	PLACE	YEAR
Lawnmower	James Edward Ransome	UK	1902
Light Bulb	Joseph Swan and Thomas Edison	UK and USA	1878
Machine Gun	James Puckle	UK	1718
Margarine	Hippolyte Megé-Mouriès	France	1868
Match	Robert Boyle	UK	1680
Mechanical Computer	Charles Babbage	UK	1835
Microscope	Zacharias Janssen	Netherlands	1590
Microwave Oven	Percy Le Baron Spencer	USA	1946
Miner's Safety Lamp	Humphry Davy	UK	1815
Motorcycle	Gottleib Daimler	Germany	1885
Nylon	Wallace H. Carothers	USA	1938
Paper Clip	Johann Vaaler	Norway	1899
Passenger Lift/ Elevator	Elisha Graves Otis	USA	1857
Pencil	Nicholas Jacques Conté	France	1795
Photographic Film	Georges Eastman	USA	1889
Pianoforte	Bartolomeo Cristofori	Italy	1720
Plastics	John W. Hyatt	USA	1868
Pneumatic Bicycle Tyre	John Boyd Dunlop	UK	1888
Pocket Calculator	Kilby, Tassel and Merryman	USA	1972

INVENTION	INVENTOR	PLACE	YEAR
Power Loom	Edmund Cartwright	UK	1785
Printing Press	Johannes Gutenberg	Germany	1450
Radar	Robert Watson-Watt	UK	1935
Razor (safety)	King Camp Gillette	USA	1895
Record (LP)	Peter Goldmark	USA	1948
Revolver	Samuel Colt	USA	1835
Safety Pin	Walter Hunt	USA	1849
Scotch Tape	Richard Drew	USA	1930
Sewing Machine	Barthelemy Thimonnier	France	1830
Skyscraper	William Le Baron Jenney	USA	1882
Spinning Jenny	James Hargreaves	UK	1764
Spinning Mule	Samuel Crompton	UK	1779
Stapler	Charles Henry Gould	UK	1868
Steam Engine (development)	James Watt	UK	1765
Steam Locomotive	Richard Trevithick	UK	1804
Steel (stainless)	Henry Brearley	UK	1913
Stethoscope	René Théophile H. Laënnec	France	1816
Submarine	Cornelius Drebbel	Netherlands	1620
Suntan Cream	Eugene Schueller	France	1936
Tank	Ernest Swinton	UK	1916
Telephone	Alexander Graham Bell	USA	1876
Telescope (reflecting)	Isaac Newton	UK	1668

INVENTION	INVENTOR	PLACE	YEAR
Telescope (refracting)	Hans Lippershey	Netherlands	1608
Television	John Logie Baird	UK	1926
Tennis	Walter G. Wingfield	UK	1873
Traffic Lights	J. P. Knight	UK	1868
Typewriter	William Burt	USA	1829
Vacuum Cleaner (electric)	Hubert Cecil Booth	UK	1901
Vending Machine	Percival Everitt	UK	1883
Washing Machine (electric)	Hurley Machine Company	USA	1908
Water Frame	Richard Arkwright	UK	1769
Radio (transatlantic)	Guglielmo Marconi	Italy	1901
Zip Fastener	Whitcomb L. Judson	USA	1893

FASCINATING FACTS

- American chemist Thomas Midgley, who developed both the environmentally deadly tetra-ethyl lead additive to petrol and chlorofluorocarbons (CFCs), died of strangulation in 1944 due to another of his inventions. Disabled from polio, he became entangled in the ropes of a system to help him out of bed.

- When British merchant Peter Durand invented the metal can in 1810, he overlooked the need for a device to open it.

- The telescope was accidentally discovered when Hans Lippershey looked through two lenses and saw that the image was magnified.

- The first rickshaw was invented in 1869 by Rev. E. Jonathan Scobie to transport his invalid wife around the streets of Yokohama.

- The Band-Aid was invented by a Johnson & Johnson employee, Earl Dickson. His wife was rather accident-prone so he devised a bandage that she could apply without help.

- The Slinky toy was the result of a failed attempt by engineer Richard James to produce an anti-vibration device for ship instruments. His goal was to develop a meter designed to monitor horsepower on naval battleships. Richard was working with tension springs when one of the springs fell to the ground. He saw how the spring kept moving after it hit the ground and an idea for a toy was born.

- Kleenex tissue was originally designed to be a gas mask filter. It was developed at the beginning of World War One to replace cotton, which was then in short supply as a surgical dressing.

- X-ray was discovered purely by accident. When German physicist Wilhelm Konrad von Roentgen was experimenting with cathode rays in 1895, he put an activated Crookes tube in a book and went out to lunch. When he returned, he discovered that a key that had also been placed in the book showed up as an image on the developed film!

FILM

TOP TEN GREATEST FILMS EVER MADE*

1   *The Shawshank Redemption* (1994)

2   *The Godfather* (1972)

3   *The Godfather: Part II* (1974)

4   *The Good, the Bad and the Ugly* (1966)

5   *Pulp Fiction* (1994)

6   *Schindler's List* (1993)

7   *12 Angry Men* (1957)

8   *One Flew Over the Cuckoo's Nest* (1975)

9   *Star Wars: Episode V – The Empire Strikes Back* (1980)

10 *The Dark Knight* (2008)

* Ordered by number of votes and reviews on www.imdb.com (Internet Movie Database).

FASCINATING FACT

- The iconic Hollywood sign is made up of 50 ft-high letters. They stand near the tip of Beachwood Canyon's Mount Lee, the highest peak in Los Angeles. The letters were built in 1923 by property developers to advertise their new sites, called Hollywoodland. It was only in the 1940s, when the film business ballooned, that the last four letters were removed.

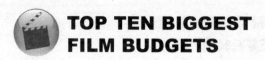

TOP TEN BIGGEST FILM BUDGETS

1	*Pirates of the Caribbean: At World's End*	Buena Vista (2007)	$300 million
2	*Spider-Man 3*	Sony (2007)	$258 million
3	*Harry Potter and the Half-Blood Prince*	Warner Bros (2009)	$250 million
4	*Avatar*	Fox (2009)	$237 million
5	*Superman Returns*	Warner Bros (2006)	$232 million
6	*Quantum of Solace*	Sony (2008)	$230 million
7	*The Chronicles of Narnia: Prince Caspian*	Buena Vista (2008)	$225 million
8	*Pirates of the Caribbean: Dead Man's Chest*	Buena Vista (2006)	$225 million
9	*Transformers: Revenge of the Fallen*	Paramount (2009)	$210 million
10	*King Kong*	Universal (2005)	$207 million

TOP TEN HIGHEST PAID ACTORS (ANNUAL EARNINGS)

1	Johnny Depp	$92 million (£72.4 million)
2	Tom Hanks	$74 million (£58.3 million)
3	Ben Stiller	$38 million (£29.9 million)
4	Brad Pitt	$35 million (£27.5 million)
5	Tom Cruise	$31 million (£24.4 million)
6	Will Smith	$31 million (£24.4 million)
7	Adam Sandler	$30 million (£23.6 million)
8	Nicole Kidman	$28 million (£22 million)
9	George Clooney	$25 million (£19.7 million)
10	Vince Vaughn	$25 million (£19.7 million)

TOP TEN HIGHEST GROSSING FILMS OF ALL TIME*

1	*Avatar*	Fox (2009)	$2.727 billion
2	*Titanic*	Paramount (1997)	$1.843 billion
3	*Lord of the Rings: The Return of the King*	New Line (2003)	$1.119 billion
4	*Pirates of the Caribbean: Dead Man's Chest*	Buena Vista (2006)	$1.066 billion
5	*Alice in Wonderland*	Buena Vista (2010)	$1.013 billion
6	*The Dark Knight*	Warner Bros (2008)	$1.001 billion
7	*Harry Potter and the Sorcerer's Stone*	Warner Bros (2001)	$0.974 billion
8	*Pirates of the Caribbean: At World's End*	Buena Vista (2007)	$0.961 billion
9	*Harry Potter and the Order of the Phoenix*	Warner Bros (2007)	$0.938 billion
10	*Harry Potter and the Half-Blood Prince*	Warner Bros (2009)	$0.934 billion

* Figures indicate worldwide box-office takings, as of June 2010.

BIGGEST WINNERS AT THE OSCARS IN THE LAST DECADE

YEAR	CEREMONY	FILM	WINS
2001	73rd Academy Awards	*Gladiator*	5
2002	74th Academy Awards	*A Beautiful Mind/ Lord of the Rings: The Fellowship of the Ring*	4
2003	75th Academy Awards	*Chicago*	6
2004	76th Academy Awards	*Lord of the Rings: The Return of the King*	11
2005	77th Academy Awards	*The Aviator*	5
2006	78th Academy Awards	*Brokeback Mountain/ King Kong/Memoirs of a Geisha*	3
2007	79th Academy Awards	*The Departed*	4
2008	80th Academy Awards	*No Country For Old Men*	4
2009	81st Academy Awards	*Slumdog Millionaire*	8
2010	82nd Academy Awards	*The Hurt Locker*	6

ACADEMY AWARD FOR BEST ACTOR IN NUMBERS

8 - The number of nominations Peter O'Toole received – making him the actor with most nominations without ever having won.

9 - The age of the youngest nominee, Jackie Cooper, for the film *Skippy*.

9 - The number of actors who tie for the most wins in the category with two each: Spencer Tracy, Fredric March, Gary Cooper, Marlon Brando, Dustin Hoffman, Tom Hanks, Jack Nicholson, Daniel Day-Lewis and Sean Penn.

9 - The number of nominations received by both Spencer Tracy and Laurence Olivier, making them the most nominated in the category.

29 - The age of the youngest winner, Adrian Brody, for the film *The Pianist*.

76 - The age of the oldest winner, Henry Fonda, for the film *On Golden Pond*.

79 - The age of the oldest nominee, Richard Farnsworth, for the film *The Straight Story*.

ACADEMY AWARD FOR BEST ACTRESS IN NUMBERS

4 - The number of awards Katherine Hepburn won – making her the actress with the most wins in the category.

6 - The number of nominations that Deborah Kerr received – making her the actress with the most nominations without ever having won.

13 - The age of the youngest nominee, Keisha Castle-Hughes, for the film *Whale Rider*.

13 - The number of nominations in the category that Meryl Streep has received – making her the actress with the most nominations in the category. (She has won twice.)

21 - The age of the youngest winner, Marlee Matlin, for the film *Children of a Lesser God*.

80 - The age of the oldest winner and nominee, Jessica Tandy, for the film *Driving Miss Daisy*.

- The record for most nominations without a single win is held by *A Turning Point* and *The Color Purple* – both were nominated for 11 Academy Awards.

- *Lord of the Rings: The Return of the King* (2003) holds the record for most Oscar nominations without a single loss (11).

- Art director Roland Anderson was nominated a record 15 times without a win. Composer Alex North also had 15 nominations without a competitive win but in 1985 received an Honorary Oscar statuette.

 # TOP TEN MOVIE VILLAINS

1	Lord Voldemort, *Harry Potter* series (2005–present) – played by Ralph Fiennes
2	Darth Vader, *Star Wars* series (1977–2005) – played by James Earl Jones, Hayden Christensen
3	Hannibal Lecter, *Silence of the Lambs* (1991) – played by Anthony Hopkins
4	The Joker, *The Dark Knight* (2008) – played by Heath Ledger
5	The Wicked Witch of the West, *The Wizard of Oz* (1939) – played by Margaret Hamilton
6	Cruella de Vil, *101 Dalmatians* (1961)
7	Annie Wilkes, *Misery* (1990) – played by Kathy Bates
8	Freddy Krueger, *A Nightmare on Elm Street* (1984) – played by Robert Englund
9	The Queen, *Snow White and the Seven Dwarfs* (1937)
10	Frank Booth, *Blue Velvet* (1986) – played by Dennis Hopper

TOP TEN SILVER SCREEN SUPERHEROES

1	Superman (Clark Kent) – played by Christopher Reeve and Brandon Routh
2	Batman (Bruce Wayne) – played by Michael Keaton, Val Kilmer, George Clooney and Christian Bale
3	Spiderman (Peter Parker) – played by Toby Maguire
4	Incredible Hulk (Bruce Banner) – played by Eric Bana and Edward Norton
5	Wolverine (Logan, from the *X-Men* series) – played by Hugh Jackman
6	Iron Man (Tony Stark) – played by Robert Downey Jr
7	Daredevil (Matt Murdock) – played by Ben Affleck
8	Green Lantern (Hal Jordan) – played by Ryan Reynolds
9	Elektra (Elektra Natchios) – played by Jennifer Garner
10	Hellboy (Anung Un Rama) – played by Ron Perlman

TOP TEN MOST QUOTED FILM LINES OF ALL TIME

	LINE	FILM
1	'I'll be back'	*The Terminator*
2	'Frankly, my dear, I don't give a damn'	*Gone With the Wind*
3	'Beam me up, Scotty'	*Star Trek*
4	'May the force be with you'	*Star Wars*
5	'Life is like a box of chocolates'	*Forrest Gump*
6	'You talking to me?'	*Taxi Driver*
7	'Show me the money'	*Jerry Maguire*
8	'Do you feel lucky, punk?'	*Dirty Harry*
9	'Here's looking at you, kid'	*Casablanca*
10	'Nobody puts Baby in the corner'	*Dirty Dancing*

TOP TEN BIGGEST BOX-OFFICE FLOPS OF ALL TIME

1   *Zyzzyx Road* (2006) - budget: $1.2 million/takings: $20

2   *Scorched* (2003) - budget: $7million/takings: $8,000

3   *D-Tox* (2002) - budget: $5.5 million/takings: $79,161

4   *My Big Fat Independent Movie* (2005) - budget: $3 million/takings: $4,655

5   *Nomad* (2007) - budget: $40 million/takings: $79,123

6   *Freaked* (1993) - budget: $12 million/takings: $29,296

7   *The Bridge of San Luis Rey* (2005) - budget: $24 million/takings: $49,981

8   *Shade* (2004) - budget: $10 million/takings: $25,032

9   *An Alan Smithee Film: Burn Hollywood Burn* (1998) - budget: $10 million/takings: $45,779

10 *Manderlay* (2006) - budget: $14.2 million/takings: $78,378

TOP TEN HIGHEST BODYCOUNTS IN A MOVIE*

	FILM	BODYCOUNTS
1	*Lord of the Rings: Return of the King: Extended Edition* (2003)	836
2	*Kingdom of Heaven: extended version* (2005)	610
3	*300* (2007)	600
4	*Troy* (2004)	572
5	*The Last Samurai* (2003)	558
6	*Lord of the Rings: The Two Towers: Extended Edition* (2002)	468
7	*Grindhouse* (2007)	310
8	*Hard Boiled* (1992)	307
9	*Titanic* (1997)	307
10	*We Were Soldiers* (2002)	305

* As of 2008.

TOP THREE LONGEST KISSES ON FILM

1   Stephanie Sherrin and Gregory Smith in *Kids in America* (2005): 5 min. 57 sec.

2   Tina Fey and Steve Carell in *Date Night* (2010): 4 min. 23 sec.

3   Jane Wyman and Regis Toomey in *You're in the Army Now* (1941): 3 min. 5 sec.

JAMES BOND FILMS IN ORDER OF NUMBER OF LEAD ACTOR APPEARANCES

ACTOR	FILMS	YEAR
Roger Moore (7)	*Live and Let Die, The Man with the Golden Gun, The Spy Who Loved Me, Moonraker, For Your Eyes Only, Octopussy, A View to a Kill*	(1973) (1974) (1977) (1979) (1981) (1983) (1985)
Sean Connery (6)	*Dr No, From Russia With Love, Goldfinger, Thunderball, You Only Live Twice, Diamonds are Forever*	(1962) (1963) (1964) (1965) (1967) (1971)
Pierce Brosnan (4)	*GoldenEye, Tomorrow Never Dies, The World is Not Enough, Die Another Day*	(1995) (1997) (1999) (2002)
Daniel Craig (2)	*Casino Royale, Quantum of Solace*	(2006) (2008)
Timothy Dalton (2)	*The Living Daylights, Licence to Kill*	(1987) (1989)
George Lazenby (1)	*On Her Majesty's Secret Service*	(1969)

- Sean Connery also starred as James Bond in *Never Say Never Again* (1983). The film is considered 'unofficial' because Eon Productions, the company behind the familiar James Bond franchise of films, did not create it. Hence the absence of such Bond film iconography as the gun barrel opening, the distinctive title sequences, or the Monty Norman-composed James Bond theme.

- The highest-grossing Bond film to date is *Casino Royale* (2006), at £594,238,532. It was also the first Bond film released in China.

 # TOP TEN ALFRED HITCHCOCK CAMEOS

1   *The 39 Steps* (1935) – As Robert Donat and Lucie Mannheim escape the theatre, he can be seen throwing away some rubbish.

2   *Rope* (1948) – His silhouette is seen on a neon sign.

3   *Dial M for Murder* (1954) – In a photograph in Grace Kelly's apartment (as part of a class reunion picture).

4   *The Man Who Knew Too Much* (1956) – Facing away from the camera, watching acrobats in the Moroccan marketplace.

5   *Vertigo* (1958) – Walking along a street.

6   *North by Northwest* (1959) – At the end of the opening credits, he just misses his bus.

7   *Psycho* (1960) – As Janet Leigh returns to her office, he is seen through the window, wearing a cowboy hat.

8   *The Birds* (1963) – Walking out of a pet shop with two white dogs (they were actually his dogs).

9   *Torn Curtain* (1966) – Sitting in a hotel lobby holding a baby.

10 *Topaz* (1969) – Being pushed in a wheelchair in an airport, until he gets up, shakes a man's hand and walks away!

FILMS IN NUMBERS

24 – The number of times that Arthur Conan-Doyle's *The Hound of the Baskervilles* has been adapted for the screen.

23,660 – The number of cinemas is the USA, making it the country with the most in the world.

127 – The number of retakes that Shelley Duvall had to do for a single scene in *The Shining*. It holds the world record.

649 – The number of times, it is thought, that the character Dracula is mentioned in all films. He is also the most depicted character in screen history, making an appearance in over 200 films.

800 – The approximate number of movies produced in India per year, twice as many as the number produced in Hollywood.

1958 – The year that Indian comic actress Manorama began her career. In 1985, she appeared in her 1000th movie, making her the most prolific lead performer in film history.

5,000 – The number of cinemas in China, meaning that there are 300,000 people to every cinema.

615,384 – The cost in dollars, *per second*, of the most expensive reel of film in history. The 26-second clip was shot by Abraham Zapruder, and shows the assassination of President Kennedy on 22 November 1963. Its total value is $16 million.

166,352 – The number of paintings exposed to the camera to create the Disney classic *Snow White and the Seven Dwarfs* (1938).

FOOD AND DRINK

TOP TEN WORLD'S MOST EXPENSIVE FOODS

	FOOD	PRICE
1	Italian White Alba Truffle	$100,000 per lb
2	Almas Caviar	$25,000 per kg
3	Yubari Melons	$26,000 for two
4	Dansuke Watermelon	$6,100 for 17 lb (7.7 kg)
5	Domenico Crolla's 'Pizza Royale 007'	$4,200
6	Samundari Khazana, the 'World's Most Expensive Curry'	$3,200
7	Wagyu Steak	$2,800
8	The Zillion Dollar Frittata	$1,000
9	The World's Most Expensive Bagel	$1,000
10	Matsutake Mushrooms	$1,000 per lb

FASCINATING FACTS

- The 'Pizza Royale 007' has the most luxurious topping in the world; including lobster marinaded in cognac, caviar soaked in champagne, smoked salmon and 24-carat flakes of edible gold!

- 'Samundari Khazana' means 'seafood treasure' – unsurprising for a curry containing crab, white truffle, caviar, quails eggs, and, you've guessed it, edible gold.

- The $1,000 Bagel from New York is topped with white truffle cream and goji berry jelly.

- In the eleventh century, the Church was opposed to the use of forks. So much so, that when a Byzantine princess who used a two-pronged gold fork died from the plague, her death was called 'a just punishment from God'.

WORLD'S BIGGEST SUPERMARKET RETAILERS*

SUPERMARKET	COUNTRY	NO. OF STORES
Wal-Mart	USA	$401,244 million (7,870+ stores)
Carrefour	France	€101,390 million (15,100+ stores)
Metro AG	Germany	€78,460 million (1,100+ stores)
Tesco	UK	£63,739 million (4,800+ stores)
Schwarz Group (Lidl)	Germany	€78,460 million (9,000+ stores)
Kroger	USA	$76,000 million (2,400+ stores)
Costco	USA	$70,977 million (560+ stores)
Aldi	Germany	€66 063 million (8,200+ stores)
Target	USA	$62,884 million (1,750+ stores)

* 2008 sales.

BIGGEST SUPERMARKETS IN THE UK*

1	Tesco	2,482
2	Sainsbury's	872
3	Morrison's	420
4	Asda	346
5	Waitrose	229

* By number of stores.

TOP FOUR COFFEE CHAINS IN THE UK*

1	Starbucks	660
2	Costa	655
3	Caffè Nero	330
4	Coffee Republic	173

* Number of outlets in 2008.

TOP TEN WORLD'S BIGGEST BEER CONSUMERS

	COUNTRY	ANNUAL NO. OF PINTS PER PERSON
1	Czech Republic	276.1
2	Ireland	230.7
3	Germany	203.7
4	Australia	193.3
5	Austria	190.5
6	United Kingdom	174.2
7	Belgium	163.6
8	Denmark	158.2
9	Finland	149.5
10	Luxembourg	148.5

TOP TEN WORLD'S SMELLIEST CHEESES*

1	Vieux Boulogne: 7-9 weeks matured
2	Pont l'Eveque: 6 weeks matured
3	Camembert de Normandie: 3 weeks matured
4	Munster: 3 weeks matured
5	Brie de Meaux 4-8 weeks matured
6	Roquefort: 3 months matured
7	Reblochon: 3-4 weeks matured
8	Livarot: 90 days matured
9	Banon: 1-2 weeks matured
10	Epoisses de Bourgogne: 4-6 weeks matured

* Cranfield University blind-tested 15 French cheeses on 19 testers and one hi-tech electronic nose developed by the university to find out which was the stinkiest.

TOP FIVE WORLD'S MOST MICHELIN-STARRED CHEFS

	CHEF	COUNTRY	NO. OF MICHELIN STARS
1	Joel Robuchon	France	25
2	Alain Ducasse	France	18
3	Gordon Ramsay	Great Britain	11
4	Thomas Keller	USA	7
5	Jean Georges	USA	4

TOP TEN WORLD'S MOST EXPENSIVE BOTTLES OF WINE AND VINTAGE

	WINE	PRICE
1	Screaming Eagle Cab (1992)	$500,000
2	Chateau Lafite (1787)	$160,000
3	Chateau Mouton Rothschild (1945)	$114,614
4	Chateau d'Yquem (1784)	$56,588
5	Massandra Sherry (1775)	$43,500
6	Romanee Conti (1990)	$28,112
7	Le Montrachet (1978)	$23,929
8	Romanée-Conti (1990)	$5,800
9	Screaming Eagle (1994)	$3,833
10	Chateau Mouton Rothschild (1982)	$700

FASCINATING FACTS

- The most expensive bottle ever, the 'Screaming Eagle Cab' was auctioned in the Napa Valley for charity.
- The Chateau Lafite and Chateau d'Yquem bottles have Thomas Jefferson's initials etched on the glass.

TOP TEN MOST COMMON FOOD ALLERGIES

1	Cow's Milk
2	Wheat Gluten
3	Soya Beans
4	Yeast
5	Corn
6	Egg Whites
7	Almonds
8	Peanuts
9	Cashew Nuts
10	Sunflower Seeds

TOP TEN MOST ANTIOXIDANT-RICH FRUITS

1	Prunes
2	Raisins
3	Blueberries
4	Blackberries
5	Strawberries
6	Raspberries
7	Plums
8	Oranges
9	Red Grapes
10	Cherries

TOP TEN MOST ANTIOXIDANT-RICH VEGETABLES

1	Kale
2	Spinach
3	Brussels Sprouts
4	Alfalfa Sprouts
5	Broccoli
6	Beetroot
7	Red Bell Peppers
8	Onions
9	Corn
10	Aubergine

FASCINATING FACT

- Did you know lemons contain more sugar than strawberries?

TOP TEN MOST TOXIC FRUIT AND VEGETABLES AFTER PESTICIDE USE

1	Peaches
2	Apples
3	Sweet Peppers
4	Celery
5	Nectarines
6	Strawberries
7	Cherries
8	Lettuce
9	Grapes
10	Pears

FASCINATING FACTS

- Iceberg lettuce got its name when California growers started to ship it covered with heaps of crushed ice in the 1920s. It had previously been called 'crisphead' lettuce.
- Archaeologists have found petrified fried cakes with holes in them, very much like the modern doughnut, in prehistoric Native American ruins. Our ancestors had a sweet tooth too!

TOP TEN WORLD'S BIGGEST FAST FOOD CHAINS

	CHAIN	NO. OF STORES
1	Subway	21,881
2	McDonald's	13,958
3	Starbucks	11,567
4	Pizza Hut	7,564
5	Burger King	7,512
6	Wendy's	6,630
7	Dunkin' Donuts	6,395
8	Taco Bell	5,588
9	KFC	5,253
10	Domino's	5,047

TOP TEN WORLD'S MOST GROWN CROPS

	CROP	NO. OF MILLION METRIC TONS PRODUCED ANNUALLY
1	Sugar Cane	1,324
2	Maize	721
3	Wheat	627
4	Rice	605
5	Potatoes	328
6	Sugar Beet	249
7	Soybean	204
8	Oil Palm Fruit	162
9	Barley	154
10	Tomato	120

TOP TEN BEST-SELLING TEA BRANDS IN THE UK

	BRAND	PERCENTAGE OF THE RETAIL MARKET
1	PG Tips	23.7 per cent
2	Tetley	22.1 per cent
3	Twinings	8.9 per cent
4	Typhoo	5.2 per cent
5	Yorkshire Tea	4 per cent
6	Lyons	1.3 per cent
7	London Fruit & Herb	1 per cent
8	Teadirect	0.8 per cent
9	Brooke Bond	0.7 per cent
10	Lift	0.6 per cent

FASCINATING FACT

- Tea bags were invented in 1904 by Thomas Sullivan in New York; he first used them to send samples to his customers instead of sealing the tea leaves in more expensive tins.

TOP TEN BEST-SELLING CONFECTIONERY IN THE UK

1	Cadbury's Dairy Milk
2	Wrigleys Extra
3	Maltesers
4	Galaxy
5	Mars Bar
6	Kit Kat
7	Celebrations
8	Quality Street
9	Haribo
10	Roses

TOP TEN WORLD'S BIGGEST CHOCOLATE CONSUMERS

	COUNTRY	ANNUAL AMOUNT CONSUMED PER PERSON
1	Switzerland	11.4 kg
2	UK	9.5 kg
3	Belgium	8.7 kg
4	Germany	8.6 kg
5	Ireland	8.1 kg
6	Denmark	7.9 kg
7	Norway	6.1 kg
8	Australia	6.0 kg
9	Poland	5.6 kg
10	USA	5.4 kg

HUNTING SEASONS IN THE UK

SEASON	DATES
Pheasant	1 October to 1 February
Partridge	1 September to 1 February
Grouse	12 August to 10 December
Duck and Goose (inland)	1 September to 31 January
Duck and Goose (below high water mark)	1 September 20 February
Chinese Water Deer	1 November to 31 March
Red Deer Stag	1 August to 30 April
Red Deer Hind	1 November to 31 March
Roe Deer Buck	1 April to 31 October
Roe Deer Doe	1 November to 31 March

TOP TEN WORLD'S BIGGEST EVER FRUITS AND VEGETABLES

	FRUIT/VEGETABLE	PLACE GROWN	WEIGHT
1	Potato	Tyre, Lebanon	11.3 kg
2	Marrow	Norfolk, England	65 kg
3	Lemon	Kefar Zeitim, Israel	5.3 kg
4	Jackfruit	Hawaii, USA	34.6 kg
5	Cabbage	Rhondda Cynon Taff, Wales	56.2 kg
6	Watermelon	Arkansas, USA	122 kg
7	Apple	Hirosaki City, Japan	1.85 kg
8	Carrot	Alaska, USA	8.61 kg
9	Pumpkin	New Jersey, USA	784.1 kg
10	Cauliflower	Alaska, USA	14.1 kg

- The tallest tomato plant ever reached an astonishing height of almost 20 metres in Lancashire, UK.
- Carrots were first cultivated in Afghanistan in the seventh century and had yellow flesh and a purple exterior. It was the Dutch who developed the orange carrot in deference to the House of Orange, and the French in the seventeenth century who most likely developed the elongated carrot, the precursor to the modern carrot.

TOP TEN WORLD'S FASTEST EATERS

1	Joey 'Jaws' Chestnut – 66 hot dogs (in buns) in 12 minutes
2	Patrick 'Deep Dish' Bertoletti – 35 dozen raw oysters in 8 minutes and 16 8-ounce corned beef sandwiches in 10 minutes
3	Takeru 'Tsunami' Kobayashi – 50 hot dogs in 12 minutes
4	Tim 'Eater X' Janus – 71 tamales in 12 minutes; 26 large cannoli in 6 minutes; 11.8 lbs of burritos in 10 minutes; 10.5 lbs of Ramen Noodles in 8 minutes; and 4 lbs of tiramisu in 6 minutes
5	'Humble' Bob Shoudt – 9.25 lbs of shoefly pie in 8 minutes; 7.6 lbs of meatballs in 12 minutes; and 25 hot dogs in 12 minutes
6	Sonya 'Black Widow' Thomas – 1 lb of cheesecake in 9 minutes
7	Hall Hunt – 63 Krystal Burgers in 8 minutes
8	'The Lovely' Juliet Lee – 13 lbs of cranberry sauce in 8 minutes
9	Tim 'Gravy' Brown – 10 lbs of cucumber and asparagus washed down with a gallon of water in less than 4 minutes
10	Richard 'The Locust' LeFevre – 5 lbs of birthday cake in 11 minutes, 26 seconds, and 247 jalapeno peppers in 8 minutes

TOP TEN MOST DANGEROUS FOODS

1	Hot dogs – to blame for 17 per cent of deaths from choking
2	Fugu – (blowfish) the internal organs contain a deadly poison
3	Ackee – ingesting the unripe fruit is poisonous, as it causes chronic vomiting that can result in coma or death
4	Peanuts – is the most dangerous food for allergy sufferers
5	Leafy Greens – unwashed greens sometimes carry a virus called Norovirus, which causes 300 deaths a year in the USA alone
6	Rhubarb – ingesting a large amount of the leaves can cause poisoning, due to the toxins they contain
7	Tuna – high mercury levels caused by pollution can be dangerous for very young and unborn children
8	Tapioca – prepared incorrectly, the cassava root (where the starch comes from) can produce cyanide
9	Coffee – can cause severe burning if mishandled
10	Mushrooms – varieties like the Death Cap, Destroying Angels and Deadly Webcap are highly poisonous

TOP TEN FOODS HIGHEST IN SATURATED FAT*

1   Hydrogenated Oils (Coconut, Palm) – 93

2   Dried Coconut – 57

3   Butter – 51

4   Rendered Animal Fats (Tallow, Suet) – 40

5   Dark Chocolate – 32

6   Fish Oil (Menhaden, Sardine) – 20-30

7   Cheese – 20

8   Nuts and Seeds (Pilinuts, Macadamia) – 9-31

9   Processed Meats (Sausage and Pâté) – 15

10 Whipped Cream – 14

* Figures show percentage of saturated fat.

FASCINATING FACTS

• Vikings used the skulls of their enemies as drinking vessels. Skol!

• Absinthe was banned in most countries in the early twentieth century, as it apparently caused madness. The reason was the presence of the toxic oil 'thujone' in wormwood, which was then one of the main ingredients of absinthe.

HISTORY

THE 12 CAESARS

	NAME	REIGN
1	Julius Caesar (102-44 BC)	49-44 BC
2	Augustus (b. 63 BC d. AD 14)	27 BC-AD 14
3	Tiberius (b. 42 BC d. AD 37)	AD 14-37
4	Gaius Caligula (AD 12-41)	AD 37-41
5	Claudius (b. 10 BC d. AD 54)	AD 41-54
6	Nero (AD 37-68)	AD 54-68
7	Galba (b. 3 BC d. AD 69)	AD 68-69
8	Otho (AD 32-69)	AD 69-69
9	Vitellius (AD 15-69)	AD 69-69
10	Vespasian (AD 9-79)	AD 69-79
11	Titus (AD 39-81)	AD 79-81
12	Domitian (AD 51-96)	AD 81-96

PREHISTORIC PERIODS

ERA	PREDOMINANT MATERIAL	PERIOD
Paleolithic (Old Stone Age)	knapped stone, wood and bone	approx. 2.5 million years ago
Mesolithic (Middle Stone Age)	flint	approx. 10,000 years ago
Neolithic (New Stone Age)	basic metal	approx. 6,000 years ago
Bronze Age	copper and tin alloy	approx. 4,000 years ago
Iron Age	iron	approx. 3,000 years ago

TOP TEN WORLD'S LONGEST WARS

| 1 | Hundred Years War, France v England: 1338–1453 (115 years) |

1 Hundred Years War, France v England: 1338–1453 (115 years)

2 Wars of the Roses, Lancaster v York: 1455–85 (30 years)

3 Thirty Years War, Catholic v Protestant: 1618–48 (30 years)

4 Peloponnesian War, Peloponnesian League v Delian League: 431–404 BC (27 years)

5 First Punic War, Rome v Carthage: 264–241 BC (23 years)

6 Napoleonic Wars, France v other European countries: 1792–1815 (23 years)

7 Greco-Persian Wars, Greece v Persia: 499–478 BC (21 years)

8 Second Great Northen War, Russia v Sweden and Baltic states: 1700–21 (21 years)

9 Vietnam War, South Vietnam (with USA support) v North Vietnam: 1957–75 (18 years)

10 Second Punic War, Rome v Carthage: 218–201 BC (17 years)

KNIGHTS OF THE ROUND TABLE*

King Arthur
Galahad
Lancelot du Lac
Gawain
Percivale
Lionel
Tristram de Lyones
Gareth
Bedivere
Bleoberis
La Cote Male Taile
Lucan
Palomides

Lamorak
Bors de Ganis
Safir
Pelleas
Kay
Ector de Maris
Dagonet
Tegyr
Brunor le Noir
Le Bel Desconneu
Alymere
Mordred

* Listed from the Winchester Round Table dating from 1270.

TOP FIVE WORLD'S LONGEST SIEGES IN HISTORY

1. Candia, Ottoman Turks besieged the Venetians: 1648–69 (21 years)
2. Khost, Afghan Mujahideen besieged Soviet Union/Afghanistan: 1980–91 (11 years)
3. Ishiyama Hongan-ji, forces of Oda Nobunaga besieged Ikkō-ikki: 1570–80 (10 years)
4. Solovetsky Monastery, Tsar's forces besieged Raskol monks: 1668–76 (8 years)
5. Harlech Castle, Yorkists besieged Lancastrians: 1461–68 (7 years)

TOP TEN WORLD'S LARGEST ARMIES*

1	China	1,600,000
2	India	1,100,000
3	North Korea	950,000
4	South Korea	560,000
5	Pakistan	550,000
6	USA	477,800
7	Vietnam	412,000
8	Turkey	402,000
9	Iraq	375,000
10	Russia	321,000

* Measured by number of staff.

TOP TEN LARGEST EMPIRES IN HISTORY

	EMPIRE	SIZE
1	British Empire (1922)	13.01 million sq miles (33.7 million sq km)
2	Mongol Empire (1270 or 1309)	12.7 million sq miles (33 million sq km)
3	Russian Empire (1866)	9.15 million sq miles (23.7 million sq km)
4	Spanish Empire (c.1740–1790)	7.7 million sq miles (20 million sq km)
5	Qing Chinese Empire (1790)	5.7 million sq miles (14.7 million sq km)
6	Yuan Dynasty (1310)	5.4 million sq miles (14 million sq km)
7	Umayyad Caliphate (720 or 750)	5 million sq miles (13 million sq km)
8	Second French Colonial Empire (1938)	4.7 million sq miles (12.3 million sq km)
9	Abbasid Caliphate (AD 750)	4.3 million sq miles (11.1 million sq km)
10	Portuguese Empire (1815)	4.2 million sq miles (10.4 million sq km)

THE FIRST COUNTRIES TO GIVE THE VOTE TO WOMEN

YEAR	COUNTRY
1893	New Zealand
1902	Australia
1906	Finland
1913	Norway
1915	Denmark and Iceland
1917	Netherlands and USSR
1918	Austria, Germany, Poland, Canada, Great Britain and Ireland
1920	USA
1921	Sweden
1929	Ecuador

TOP FIVE UK'S LONGEST REIGNING MONARCHS

1   Queen Victoria – 63 years
2   King George III – 59 years
3   Queen Elizabeth II – 58 years and counting
4   King James I – 58 years
5   King Henry III – 56 years

THE LINE OF SUCCESSION TO THE BRITISH THRONE

1   HRH Prince Charles, Prince of Wales (b. 1948)

2   HRH Prince William of Wales, eldest son of Prince Charles (b. 1982)

3   HRH Prince Henry of Wales, youngest son of Prince Charles
    (b. 1984)

4   HRH Prince Andrew, The Duke of York, second son of HM Queen
    Elizabeth II (b. 1960)

5   HRH Princess Beatrice of York, elder daughter of Prince Andrew
    (b. 1988)

6   HRH Princess Eugenie of York, younger daughter of Prince Andrew
    (b. 1990)

7   HRH Prince Edward, Earl of Wessex, youngest son of HM Queen
    Elizabeth II (b. 1964)

8   HRH Prince James of Wessex, Viscount Severn, son of Prince
    Edward (b. 2007)

9   Lady Louise Alice Elizabeth Mary Mountbatten Windsor, daughter
    of Prince Edward (b. 2003)

10 HRH Princess Anne, The Princess Royal, only daughter of HM Queen
    Elizabeth II (b. 1950)

KINGS AND QUEENS OF ENGLAND

MONARCH	YEAR ASCENDED TO THE THRONE
NORMAN	
William I	1066
William II	1087
Henry I	1100
Stephen	1135
PLANTAGENET	
Henry II	1154
Richard I	1189
John	1199
Henry III	1216
Edward I	1272
Edward II	1307
Edward III	1327
Richard II	1377
LANCASTER	
Henry IV	1399
Henry V	1413
Henry VI	1422
YORK	
Edward IV	1461
Edward V	1483
Richard III	1483

TUDOR

Henry VII	1485
Henry VIII	1509
Edward VI	1547
Mary I	1553
Elizabeth I	1558

STUART

James I	1603
Charles I	1625
Oliver Cromwell	The Interregnum 1649
Charles II	1660
James II	1685
William III and Mary II	1688
Anne	1702

HANOVER

George I	1714
George II	1727
George III	1760
George IV	1820
William IV	1830
Victoria	1837

SAXE-COBURG-GOTHA

Edward VII	1901

WINDSOR

George V	1910
Edward VIII	1936
George VI	1936
Elizabeth II	1952

A VERSE TO HELP REMEMBER ALL THIS

Willie, Willie, Harry, Steve,
Harry, Dick, John, Harry three;
Edward One, Two, Three, Dick two,
Henry four, five, six... then who?
Edward four, five, Dick the Bad,
Harrys (twain), Ned six (the Lad)
Mary, Lizzie, James the Vain,
Then Charlie, Charlie, James again.
William and Mary, Anne o'Gloria,
Georges four, Will four, Victoria;
Eddie, Georgie, Ned the eighth;
George the sixth, Elizabeth.

KEY DATES IN BRITISH HISTORY

DATES (AD)	EVENT
43	Roman Emperor Claudius invades Britain
61	Revolt by Queen Boudicca of the Iceni tribe against the Romans
122-26	Construction of Hadrian's Wall
435	Britain invaded by Angles, Saxons and Jutes
597	St Augustine lands in Kent (AD 602 founds Canterbury Cathedral and becomes first Archbishop of Canterbury)
782-3	Construction of Offa's Dyke
793	First Viking raid on Britain
823	Egbert King of Wessex acknowledged as overlord of all England
1040	Macbeth slays Duncan
1066	William the Conqueror defeats Harold Godwinson at the Battle of Hastings and is crowned king
1086	Domesday Book completed

DATES (AD)	EVENT
1170	Murder of Thomas à Beckett in the Canterbury Cathedral
1215	King John signs the Magna Carta at Runnymede, 15 June
1216	Llywelyn the Great is de facto ruler of Wales
1314	Robert Bruce defeats the English
1415	Battle of Agincourt, victory for Henry V
1453	End of Hundred Years War (1337-1453)
1485	Battle of Bosworth Field (Wars of the Roses 1455-85)
1513	Battle of Flodden (James IV of Scotland killed)
1536	Anne Boleyn executed and Thomas Cromwell dissolves monasteries
1587	Execution of Mary, Queen of Scots
1588	Spanish Armada defeated
1611	King James Bible (authorised version of the Bible)
1642	English Civil War begins, Battle of Edgehill
1645	Battle of Naseby
1649	Charles I executed
1660	Restoration of Monarchy under Charles II
1665	Great Plague of London
1666	Great Fire of London
1690	Battle of the Boyne (James II defeated in Ireland)
1692	Massacre of Glencoe
1707	Act of Union
1746	Battle of Culloden Moor
1775	American War of Independence
1801	Union of Great Britain and Ireland
1807	Slave trade abolished in British Empire
1825	First railway opened, Stockton to Darlington
1834	'Tolpuddle martyrs' deported to Australia for seven years
1840	Penny Postage instituted, Opium War against China declared
1851	Great Exhibition in Hyde Park – Crystal Palace

DATES (AD)	EVENT
1854	Charge of the Light Brigade during Crimean War
1857	Indian Mutiny, Relief of Lucknow
1879	Zulu War, Tay Bridge disaster
1899	Boer War
1914	Franz Ferdinand assassinated at Sarajevo and World War One begins
1916	Battles of Verdun, Jutland and the Somme
1918	Armistice Day, women over 30 get the vote
1921	Irish Free State set up
1939	Germany invades Poland and World War Two begins
1940	Dunkirk evacuated Battle of Britain
1944	D-Day landings by allies 6 June
1945	World War Two ends
1953	Edmund Hillary and Sherpa Tenzing reach Everest summit
1954	Food rationing ends in Britain
1964	Last man hanged in UK
1971	Decimalisation of currency
1973	Britain joins the Common Market
1982	Falklands War begins
1990	Margaret Thatcher resigns as Prime Minister after 11 years, 209 days in office
1991	First Gulf War begins in Iraq
1994	Official opening of the Channel Tunnel
1997	Diana, Princess of Wales, killed in car crash
1998	The Good Friday Agreement
2002	The Queen Mother dies aged 101
2003	Second Gulf War in Iraq
2005	Terrorists explode bombs on London Transport System
2008	Boris Johnson becomes new Mayor of London
2010	First coalition government since 1945

THE SEVEN WONDERS OF THE ANCIENT WORLD

1   Pyramids, Giza*

2   Hanging Gardens of Babylon

3   Temple of Artemis, Ephesus

4   Statue of Zeus, Olympia

5   Mausoleum at Halicarnassus

6   Colossus of Rhodes

7   Pharos Lighthouse, Alexandria

* Only the Pyramids can still be seen today.

FASCINATING FACTS

- The Battle of Hastings did not take place in Hastings, but was actually fought at Senlac Hill, about six miles north-west of Hastings.
- In Ancient Egypt the heart was considered to be the seat of intelligence – not the brain.
- During the last 3,500 years, it is estimated that the world has had a grand total of 230 years in which no wars took place.
- In Ancient Egypt, cats were considered sacred. When a family pet cat died, the entire family would shave off their eyebrows and remain in mourning until they had grown back.

EVOLUTION OF THE 'HOMO' SPECIES

Homo habilis (Handy Man): 2.5-1.5 million years ago

Homo rudolfensis (Rudolph Man): 1.9 million years ago

Homo georgicus (Georgia Man): 1.8-1.6 million years ago

Homo ergaster (Working Man): 1.9-1.25 million years

Homo erectus (Upright Man): *c.* 1.25-0.3 million years ago

Homo cepranensis (Ceprano Man): *c.* 0.8 million years ago

Homo antecessor (Predecessor Man): 0.8-0.35 million years ago

Homo heidelbergensis (Heidelberg Man): 0.67-0.25 million years ago

Homo neanderthalensis (Neanderthal Man): 0.23-0.03 million years ago

Homo rhodesiensis (Rhodesia Man): 0.3-0.12 million years ago

Homo sapiens idaltu (Elderly Wise Man): 0.16 million years ago

Homo floresiensis (Flores Man): 0.10-0.012 million years ago

Homo sapiens: 0.25 million years ago to present

LANGUAGE

TOP TEN WORLD'S MOST WIDELY SPOKEN LANGUAGES*

1	Chinese Mandarin	1 billion+
2	English	512 million
3	Hindi	501 million
4	Spanish	399 million
5	Russian	285 million
6	Arabic	265 million
7	Bengali	245 million
8	Portuguese	196 million
9	Malay-Indonesian	140 million
10	Japanese	125 million

* Native speakers.

TOP TEN WORLD'S MOST DIFFICULT LANGUAGES

1	Tuyuca, Eastern Amazon	50-140 noun classes or genders
2	Kwaio, Central Malaita	Solomon Islands
3	!Xóõ or Taa, Botswana/Namibia	A Khoisan language with 17 vowel sounds and five basic clicks
4	Ubykh, Manyas region of Turkey	78 consonant sounds, now a dead language
5	Bora, Peru/Colombia	350 noun classes or genders
6	Chindali, Niger-Congo	A Bantu language
7	Berik, New Guinea	Belonging to the Tor-Kwerba language
8	Kuuk-Thaayorre, North Australia	A Paman language, only 250 speakers in 2006
9	Dyirbal, Queensland, Australia	Branch of the Pama-Nyungan family, possibly less than five speakers
10	Estonian	14 cases of grammar

TOP TEN PANGRAMS*

1   Waltz, bad nymph, for quick jigs vex. (28 letters)
2   Brick quiz whangs jumpy veldt fox. (28 letters)
3   Quick zephyrs blow, vexing daft Jim. (29 letters)
4   Sphinx of black quartz, judge my vow. (29 letters)
5   Two driven jocks help fax my big quiz. (30 letters)
6   Five quacking zephyrs jolt my wax bed. (31 letters)
7   The five boxing wizards jump quickly. (31 letters)
8   Pack my box with five dozen liquor jugs. (32 letters)
9   The quick brown fox jumps over the lazy dog. (35 letters)
10 Jinxed wizards pluck ivy from the big quilt. (36 letters)

* A sentence that includes every letter of the alphabet at least once.

 TOP TEN MOST COMMONLY USED WORDS IN THE ENGLISH LANGUAGE

1   the
2   of
3   and
4   a
5   to
6   in
7   is
8   you
9   that
10 it

TOP TEN NEWEST ADDITIONS TO THE DICTIONARY*

1. arf – interjection – the sound of a dog's bark, or a human imitating a dog's bark

2. Generation Y – noun – the generation of people following Generation X – noun – esp. regarded as having attitudes or values which are in direct contrast to those of the preceding generation

3. re-rub – noun – musical term meaning remix

4. superbug – noun – an insect that is resistant to insecticides and a bacterium that is resistant to antibiotics

5. techy – adjective – i) technologically sophisticated or complicated and ii) of music, influenced by techno

6. 3G – adjective – (of telephone technology) third-generation

7. blogosphere – noun – informal personal websites and weblogs collectively

8. adultescent – noun – an adult who has retained the interests, behaviour and lifestyle of an adolescent

9. bum rap – noun – unjust criticism

10. Beatlesque – adjective – characteristic or reminiscent of The Beatles

* Words added between December 2009 and March 2010.

COLLECTORS AND COLLECTIONS

COLLECTOR	COLLECTION
Arctophile	Teddy bears
Bibliophile	Books
Campanarian	Bells
Cartophilist	Cigarette cards
Cochlearist	Spoons
Conchologist	Shells
Deltiologist	Postcards
Digitabulist	Thimbles
Fromologist	Cheese labels
Grabatologist	Ties
Lepidopterist	Butterflies/Moths
Numismatist	Coins
Philatelist	Stamps
Phillumenist	Matchbox labels
Tegestologist	Beer mats
Vintitulist	Wine labels

 # THE GREEK ALPHABET

A α: Alpha
B β: Beta
Γ γ: Gamma
Δ δ: Delta
E ε: Epsilon
Z ζ: Zeta
H η: Eta
Θ θ: Theta
I ι: Iota
K κ: Kappa

Λ λ: Lambda
M μ: Mu
N ν: Nu
Ξ ξ: Xi
O o: Omicron
Π π: Pi
P ρ: Rho
Σ σ: Sigma
T τ: Tau
Y υ: Upsilon

Φ φ: Phi
X x: Chi
Ψ ψ: Psi
Ω ω: Omega

THE PHONETIC ALPHABET

Alpha	Golf	Mike	Sierra	Yankee
Bravo	Hotel	November	Tango	Zulu
Charlie	India	Oscar	Uniform	
Delta	Juliet	Papa	Victor	
Echo	Kilo	Quebec	Whisky	
Foxtrot	Lima	Romeo	X-ray	

LANGUAGE FAMILIES AND NUMBER OF SPEAKERS

LANGUAGE FAMILIES	NUMBER OF SPEAKERS
Indo-European	2,000,000,000
Sino-Tibetan	1,040,000,000
Niger-Congo	260,000,000
Afro-Asiatic	230,000,000
Austronesian	200,000,000
Davidian	140,000,000
Japanese	120,000,000
Altaic	90,000,000
Austro-Asiatic	60,000,000
Korean	60,000,000
Tai	50,000,000
Nilo-Saharan	30,000,000
Amerindian (North, Central, South America)	25,000,000
Uralic	23,000,000
Miao-Yao	7,000,000
Caucasian	6,000,000
Indo-Pacific	3,000,000
Khoisan	50,000
Australian aborigine	50,000
Palaeosiberian	25,000

LATIN PHRASES COMMONLY USED IN ENGLISH

LATIN PHRASE	ENGLISH TRANSLATION
Ad hoc	'towards this', for this special purpose
Ad infinitum	'to infinity', endless repetition
Ad nauseam	'to the point of sickness', endlessly repetitive
A priori	'from the previous', deductive reasoning
Bona fides	'good faith', genuineness
Carpe diem	'seize the day', enjoy the moment
Compos mentis	'having control of one's mind', sane
Curriculum vitae	'course of life', outline of qualifications and experience
Et al	'and other things'
Ex gratia	'from favour', given as a favour
Habeas corpus	'you should have the body', maintains the right of the subject to protection from unlawful imprisonment
In camera	'in the room', secret
In extremis	'in the last', in desperate circumstances
In flagrante delecto	'with the crime blazing', actually committing the crime
Infra dig	'below dignity', below one's dignity
In loco parentis	'in place of a parent'
In vitro	'in glass', in a test tube
Ipso facto	'by the fact itself', thereby
Mea culpa	'through my fault', expression of repentance
Non sequitur	'it does not follow', an illogical step in an argument
Nota bene	'note well', often abbreviated as NB
Per capita	'by heads', per head of the population
Prima facie	'at first sight', on the evidence available
Quid pro quo	'something for something', retaliation
Quod erat demonstrandum	'which was to be shown', often used as QED
Sine qua non	'without which not', an indispensable condition

PHOBIAS

Acrophobia	fear of heights
Agoraphobia	fear of open spaces
Ailourophobia	fear of cats
Algophobia	fear of pain
Androphobia	fear of men
Apiphobia	fear of bees
Arachnophobia	fear of spiders
Astraphobia	fear of lightning
Bibliophobia	fear of books
Brontophobia	fear of thunder
Claustrophobia	fear of enclosed spaces
Cynophobia	fear of dogs
Dendrophobia	fear of trees
Ergasiophobia	fear of work
Gametophobia	fear of marriage
Gymnophobia	fear of nudity
Gynophobia	fear of women
Haematophobia	fear of blood
Hippophobia	fear of horses
Hydrophobia	fear of water
Lalophobia	fear of speech
Linonophobia	fear of string
Musophobia	fear of mice
Nosophobia	fear of disease
Nyctophobia	fear of darkness
Ombrophobia	fear of rain
Oneirophobia	fear of dreams
Ophidiophobia	fear of snakes
Ornithophobia	fear of birds
Phasmophobia	fear of ghosts

Phonophobia	fear of noise/speaking aloud
Pteraphobia	fear of flying
Pyrophobia	fear of fire
Sciophobia	fear of shadows
Teratophobia	fear of monsters
Triskaidekaphobia	fear of the number 13
Xenophobia	fear of foreigners
Zoophobia	fear of animals

FASCINATING FACTS

- There are more than 2,700 spoken languages in the world. In addition, there are more than 7,000 dialects.
- All pilots on international flights identify themselves in English.
- Somalia is the only African country in which the entire population speaks the same language, Somali.
- More than 1,000 different languages are spoken on the continent of Africa. Many languages in Africa include a 'click' sound that is pronounced at the same time as other sounds.

LITERATURE

TOP TEN BEST-SELLING BOOKS OF ALL TIME*

1	*The Bible*		6 billion
2	*Quotations from Chairman Mao Zedong*	Mao Zedong	900 million
3	*The Qur'an*		800 million
4	*Xinhua Zidian*		400 million
5	*The Book of Mormon*	Joseph Smith Jr	120 million
6	*Harry Potter and the Philosopher's Stone*	J. K. Rowling	107 million
7	*And Then There Were None*	Agatha Christie	100 million
8	*The Lord of the Rings*	J. R. R. Tolkien	100 million
9	*Harry Potter and the Half-Blood Prince*	J. K. Rowling	65 million
10	*The Da Vinci Code*	Dan Brown	65 million

* Information compiled in 2007.

TOP TEN MOST TRANSLATED AUTHORS*

1	Walt Disney Productions
2	Agatha Christie
3	Jules Verne
4	William Shakespeare
5	Enid Blyton
6	Vladmir Lenin
7	Barbara Cartland
8	Danielle Steel
9	Hans Christian Anderson
10	Stephen King

* Last updated September 2004.

TOP TEN BEST-SELLING BOOKS IN THE UK 2001–2010

	TITLE	AUTHOR
1	*Harry Potter and the Deathly Hallows*	J. K. Rowling
2	*Harry Potter and the Half-Blood Prince*	J. K. Rowling
3	*Breaking Dawn*	Stephenie Meyer
4	*Twilight*	Stephenie Meyer
5	*Eclipse*	Stephenie Meyer
6	*The Tales of Beedle the Bard*	J. K. Rowling
7	*New Moon*	Stephenie Meyer
8	*The Time Traveller's Wife*	Audrey Niffenegger
9	*The Kite Runner*	Khaled Hosseini
10	*A Thousand Splendid Suns*	Khaled Hosseini

TOP TEN BEST-SELLING AUTHORS IN THE UK 2001–2010

1	J. K. Rowling
2	Stephenie Meyer
3	Julia Donaldson
4	Terry Pratchett
5	Jamie Oliver
6	Dan Brown
7	Enid Blyton
8	Bernard Cornwell
9	Alexander McCall Smith
10	William Shakespeare

TOP TEN BEST-SELLING AUTHORS OF ALL TIME*

1	Agatha Christie	2 billion
2	Barbara Cartland	1 billion
3	Harold Robbins	750 million
4	Georges Simenon	700 million
5	Danielle Steel	560 million
6	Gilbert Patten	500 million
7	Leo Tolstoy	413 million
8	J. K. Rowling	400 million
9	Jackie Collins	400 million
10	Horatio Alger	400 million

* Copies sold.

FASCINATING FACT

- The politically motivated ban of *Nineteen-Eighty-Four* in the USSR lasted for 40 years until 1990 – roughly the duration of the Cold War.

TOP TEN BANNED LITERARY CLASSICS*

1 *Ulysses* – James Joyce: reason of obscenity in 1922

2 *The Adventures of Huckleberry Finn* – Mark Twain: reason of 'racial depictions' as recently as 2001

3 *Candide* – Voltaire: reason of obscenity in 1930

4 *Brave New World* – Aldous Huxley: reason of its presentation of drugs and promiscuity, and its general dystopian outlook in 1932

5 *Nineteen-Eighty-Four* – George Orwell: reason of its political views and dystopian theme in 1950

6 *The Catcher in the Rye* – J. D. Salinger: reason of its profanity and portrayal of teenage sexuality and angst in 1985

7 *Of Mice and Men* – John Steinbeck: for many reasons, but often cited are its apparent sexism and racism, and its pro-euthanasia, liberal stance in 1953

8 *Slaughterhouse-Five* – Kurt Vonnegut: reason of controversial subject matter and profanity in 1975

9 *Uncle Tom's Cabin* – Harriet B. Stowe: reason of its anti-slavery stance in 1852

10 *Lord of the Flies* – William Golding: reason of its portrayal of the disintegration of human morals, and religion in 1992

* Dated from the year it was first banned.

TOP TEN NOVELISTIC ONE-HIT WONDERS

	AUTHOR	TITLE
1	Harper Lee	*To Kill a Mockingbird*
2	Margaret Mitchell	*Gone With the Wind*
3	Emily Brontë	*Wuthering Heights*
4	J.D. Salinger	*The Catcher in the Rye*
5	Oscar Wilde	*The Picture of Dorian Gray*
6	John Kennedy O'Toole	*A Confederacy of Dunces*
7	Sylvia Plath	*The Bell Jar*
8	Anna Sewell	*Black Beauty*
9	Boris Pasternak	*Dr Zhivago*
10	Arundhati Roy	*The God of Small Things*

LITERARY FIRSTS

The first history book, the *Great Universal History*, was published by Rashid-Eddin of Persia in 1311.

The first novel, called *The Story of Genji*, was written in 1007 by Japanese noblewoman, Murasaki Shikibu.

The first novel sold through a vending machine (at the Paris Métro) was *Murder on the Orient Express*.

The first English dictionary was written by Samuel Johnson in 1755.

The first novel to be written on a typewriter was *Life on the Mississippi*, written by Mark Twain in 1883.

The first printed book, a copy of the Buddhist *Diamond Sutra* was produced in China using carved wooden blocks to print the text on paper.

BOOKER PRIZE WINNERS (UK)

YEAR	AUTHOR	BOOK TITLE
1980	William Golding	*Rites of Passage*
1981	Salman Rushdie	*Midnight's Children*
1982	Thomas Keneally	*Schindler's Ark*
1983	J. M. Coetzee	*Life and Times of Michael K*
1984	Anita Brookner	*Hotel du Lac*
1985	Keri Hulme	*The Bone People*
1986	Kingsley Amis	*The Old Devils*
1987	Penelope Lively	*Moon Tiger*
1988	Peter Carey	*Oscar and Lucinda*
1989	Kazuo Ishiguro	*Remains of the Day*
1990	A. S. Byatt	*Possession*
1991	Ben Okri	*The Famished Road*
1992	Barry Unsworth	*Sacred Hunger*
	Michael Ondaatje	*The English Patient*
1993	Roddy Doyle	*Paddy Clarke Ha Ha Ha*
1994	James Kelman	*How Late it Was How Late*
1995	Pat Barker	*The Ghost Road*
1996	Graham Swift	*Last Orders*
1997	Arundhati Roy	*The God of Small Things*
1998	Ian McEwan	*Amsterdam*
1999	J. M. Coetzee	*Disgrace*
2000	Margaret Atwood	*The Blind Assassin*
2001	Peter Carey	*True History of the Kelly Gang*
2002	Yann Martel	*Life of Pi*
2003	DBC Pierre	*Vernon God Little*
2004	Alan Hollinghurst	*The Line of Beauty*
2005	John Banville	*The Sea*
2006	Kiran Desai	*The Inheritance of Loss*

2007	Anne Enright	*The Gathering*
2008	Aravind Adiga	*The White Tiger*
2009	Hilary Mantel	*Wolf Hall*

PULITZER PRIZE FOR FICTION WINNERS (US)

YEAR	AUTHOR	BOOK TITLE
1980	Norman Mailer	*The Executioner's Song*
1981	John Updike	*Rabbit is Rich*
1983	Alice Walker	*The Color Purple*
1984	William Kennedy	*Ironweed*
1985	Alison Lurie	*Foreign Affairs*
1986	Larry McMurtry	*Lonesome Dove*
1987	Peter Taylor	*A Summons to Memphis*
1988	Toni Morrison	*Beloved*
1989	Anne Tyler	*Breathing Lessons*
1990	Oscar Hijuelos	*The Mambo Kings Play Songs of Love*
1991	John Updike	*Rabbit at Rest*
1992	Jane Smiley	*A Thousand Acres*
1993	Robert Olen Butler	*A Good Scent from a Strange Mountain*
1994	E. Annie Proulx	*The Shipping News*
1995	Carol Shields	*The Stone Diaries*
1996	Richard Ford	*Independence Day*
1997	Steven Millhouser	*Martin Dressler: The Tale of an American Dreamer*
1998	Philip Roth	*American Pastoral*
1999	Michael Cunningham	*The Hours*
2000	Jhumpa Lahiri	*Interpreter of Maladies*
2001	Michael Chabon	*The Amazing Adventures of Kavalier & Clay*
2002	Richard Russo	*Empire Falls*

2003	Jeffrey Eugenides	*Middlesex*
2004	Edward P. Jones	*The Known World*
2005	Marilynne Robinson	*Gilead*
2006	Geraldine Brooks	*March*
2007	Cormac McCarthy	*The Road*
2008	Junot Diaz	*The Brief Wondrous Life of Oscar Wao*
2009	Elizabeth Strout	*Oliver Kitteridge*
2010	Paul Harding	*Tinkers*

POETS LAUREATE

(Post not officially established until 1668)

YEAR APPOINTED	POET
1617	Ben Jonson
1638	Sir William Davenant
1668	John Dryden
1689	Thomas Shadwell
1692	Nahum Tate
1715	Nicholas Rowe
1718	Laurence Eusden
1730	Colley Cibber
1757	William Whitehead
1785	Thomas Warton
1790	Henry Pye
1813	Robert Southey
1843	William Wordsworth
1850	Alfred Lord Tennyson
1896	Alfred Austin
1913	Robert Bridges
1930	John Masefield
1968	Cecil Day Lewis

1972	Sir John Betjeman
1984	Ted Hughes
1999	Andrew Motion
2009	Carol Ann Duffy

REFUSALS OF THE POST

YEAR	POET
1757	Thomas Gray
1785	William Mason
1813	Sir Walter Scott
1896	William Morris
1984	Philip Larkin

 # LITERARY PSEUDONYMS

PSEUDONYM	REAL NAME
Agatha Christie	Mary Westmacott
Anne Rice	Howard Allen O'Brian
Artemus Ward	Charles Farrar Browne
Barbara Cartland	Barbara McCorquodale
Barbara Vine	Barbara Grasemann
Boz	Charles Dickens
Daniel Defoe	Daniel Foe
Doctor Seuss	Theodore Seuss Geisel
Ed McBain	Evan Hunter
Elizabeth Peters	Barbara Mertz
George Eliot	Mary Ann Evans
George Orwell	Eric Arthur Blair
George Sand	Amandine-Aurore Lucil le Dupin
Harold Robbins	Harold Rubin

Jack Higgins	Harry Patterson
Jack London	John Griffith
James Herriot	James Alfred Wight
John Beynon	John Wyndham Parkes Lucas Beynon Harris
John le Carré	David John Moore Cornwell
John Wyndham	John Wyndham Parkes Lucas Beynon Harris
Joseph Conrad	Jozef Teodor Nalecz Konrad Korzeniowski
Lewis Carroll	Charles Lutwidge Dodgson
Mark Twain	Samuel Langhorne Clemens
Mickey Spillane	Frank Morrison
Molière	Jean-Baptiste Poquelin
Paul Klenousky	Sir Henry Wood
Ruth Rendell	Barbara Grasemann
Stephen King	Richard Bachman
Tennessee Williams	Thomas Lanier
Tom Stoppard	Tomas Straussler
Virgil	Publius Vergilus Maro
Voltaire	Francois-Marie Arouet
W. C. Fields	Mahatma Kane Jeeves
Woody Allen	Allen Stewart Konigsberg

 TOP TEN FAMOUS FIRST LINES

1. 'All happy families are alike; each unhappy family is unhappy in its own way.' Leo Tolstoy, *Anna Karenina*

2. 'It is a truth universally acknowledged that a single man in possession of a good fortune must be in want of a wife.' Jane Austen, *Pride and Prejudice*

3. 'It was the best of times, it was the worst of times...' Charles Dickens, *A Tale of Two Cities*

4 'Last night I dreamt I went to Manderley again.'
Daphne du Maurier, *Rebecca*

5 'As Gregor Samsa awoke one morning from uneasy dreams he
found himself transformed in his bed into a gigantic insect.'
Franz Kafka, *The Metamorphosis*

6 'It was a bright cold day in April, and the clocks were striking
thirteen.' George Orwell, *Nineteen-Eighty-Four*

7 'I have just returned from a visit to my landlord, the solitary
neighbour that I shall be troubled with.'
Emily Brontë, *Wuthering Heights*

8 'Midway in our life's journey, I went astray from the straight road
and woke to find myself alone in a dark wood.' Dante's *Inferno*

9 'When shall we three meet again

In thunder, lightning, or in rain?' William Shakespeare, *Macbeth*

10 'My mother died today, or perhaps it was yesterday.'
Albert Camus, *L'Étranger*

TOP TEN BRITAIN'S
BEST-LOVED POETS

1	T. S. Eliot
2	John Donne
3	Benjamin Zephaniah
4	Wilfred Owen
5	Philip Larkin
6	William Blake
7	W. B. Yeats
8	John Betjeman
9	John Keats
10	Dylan Thomas

TOP TEN LONGEST NOVELS IN THE ENGLISH LANGUAGE

	TITLE	AUTHOR	WORD COUNT
1	*Mission Earth*	L. Ron Hubbard	1.2 million words
2	*Sironia, Texas*	Madison Cooper	1.1 million words
3	*Clarissa*	Samuel Richardson	969,000 words
4	*Poor Fellow My Country*	Xavier Herbert	850,000 words
5	*Miss MacIntosh, My Darling*	Marguerite Young	700,000 words
6	*A Suitable Boy*	Vikram Seth	593,674 words
7	*Atlas Shrugged*	Ayn Rand	565,223 words
8	*Remembrance Rock*	Carl Sandburg	532,030 words
9	*Gai-Jin*	James Clavell	487,700 words
10	*Infinite Jest*	David Foster Wallace	484,001 words

LITERATURE IN NUMBERS

The longest non-fiction book – *The Yongle Dadian*, 10,000 volumes (only 100 survive)
The most prolific author – Barbara Cartland – 723 novels in her lifetime
The biggest first print run – *Harry Potter and the Deathly Hallows*, 12 million copies in 2007
The longest sentence in a novel – comprising 823 words, 93 commas, 51 semicolons and four dashes in Victor Hugo's *Les Misérables*

THE HARRY POTTER BOOKS

TITLE	YEAR PUBLISHED	FIRST PRINT RUN IN USA
The Philosopher's Stone	June 1997	50,000
The Chamber of Secrets	July 1998	250,000
The Prisoner of Azkaban	July 1999	500,000
The Goblet of Fire	July 2000	3.8 million
The Order of the Phoenix	June 2003	6.8 million
The Half-Blood Prince	July 2005	10.8 million
The Deathly Hallows	July 2007	12 million

MUSIC

TOP TEN BEST-SELLING ARTISTS OF ALL TIME

	ARTIST	NO. OF ALBUMS SOLD
1	Elvis Presley	over 1 billion
2	The Beatles	over 750 million
3	Michael Jackson	over 750 million
4	Frank Sinatra	over 500 million
5	Abba	370 million
6	Led Zeppelin	over 300 million
7	Nana Mouskouri	300 million
8	Queen	300 million
9	Tino Rossi	300 million
10	Julio Iglesias	250 million

UK MUSIC RECORD SALES CERTIFICATIONS

DISC	SINGLE SALES	ALBUM SALES
Silver	200,000	60,000
Gold	400,000	100,000
Platinum	600,000	300,000
Multi-platinum	1.2 million	600,000

TOP TEN MOST COVERED SONGS

	SONG TITLE	ARTIST
1	'Eleanor Rigby'	The Beatles
2	'Yesterday'	The Beatles
3	'Cry Me a River'	Julie London
4	'And I Love Her'	The Beatles
5	'(I Can't Get No) Satisfaction'	The Rolling Stones
6	'Imagine'	John Lennon
7	'Summertime'	Abbie Mitchell
8	'Blackbird'	The Beatles
9	'Over the Rainbow'	Judy Garland
10	'The Look of Love'	Dusty Springfield

TOP TEN MOST COVERED SONGWRITERS

1	John Lennon
2	Paul McCartney
3	Traditional*
4	Bob Dylan
5	Richard Rodgers
6	Ira Gershwin
7	Burt Bacharach
8	Cole Porter
9	George Gershwin
10	Hal David

* Traditional constitutes well-known songs that are not copyrighted.

LONGEST CONCERT TOURS

1   Cher's Living Proof: The Farewell Tour
    (14 June 2002 to 30 April 2005) 325 shows

2   Bon Jovi's New Jersey Syndicate Tour
    (30 October 1988 to 17 February 1990) 232 Shows

3   Aerosmith's Nine Lives Tour
    (8 May 1997 to 17 July 1999) 204 shows

4   Guns N' Roses' Use Your Illusion Tour
    (24 May 1991 to 17 July 1993) 192 shows

TEN YEARS OF CHRISTMAS NUMBER ONES

YEAR	SONG TITLE	ARTIST
2000	'Can We Fix It?'	Bob the Builder
2001	'Somethin' Stupid'	Robbie Williams and Nicole Kidman
2002	'Sound of the Underground'	Girls Aloud
2003	'Mad World'	Michael Andrews (feat. Gary Jules)
2004	'Do They Know It's Christmas?'	Band Aid 20
2005	'That's My Goal'	Shayne Ward
2006	'A Moment Like This'	Leona Lewis
2007	'When You Believe'	Leon Jackson
2008	'Hallelujah'	Alexandra Burke
2009	'Killing in the Name'	Rage Against the Machine

UK BEST-SELLING RECORDS OF THE YEAR (LAST TEN YEARS)

YEAR	SONG TITLE	ARTIST
2000	'Can We Fix It?'	Bob the Builder
2001	'It Wasn't Me'	Shaggy feat. RikRok
2002	'Anything is Possible/Evergreen'	Will Young
2003	'Where is the Love?'	The Black Eyed Peas
2004	'Do They Know it's Christmas?'	Band Aid 20
2005	'Is This the Way to Amarillo?'	Tony Christie feat. Peter Kay
2006	'Crazy'	Gnarls Barkley
2007	'Bleeding Love'	Leona Lewis
2008	'Hallelujah'	Alexandra Burke
2009	'Poker Face'	Lady Gaga

TOP TEN BIGGEST CONCERT ATTENDANCES

1. Rod Stewart at Copacabana Beach, Rio (31 December 1994) – 3.5 million
2. New York Philharmonic in Central Park, New York (5 July 1986) – 800,000
3. Garth Brooks in Central Park, New York (7 August 1997) 750,000
4. Steve Wozniak's 1983 USA Festival (28-30 May 1983) – 670,000
5. Summer Jam at Watkins Glen, New York (28 July 1973) 600,000+
6. Isle of Wight Festival (1970) – 600,000
7. Simon and Garfunkel in Central Park, New York (19 September 1981) – 500,000
8. Toronto SARS Benefit (30 July 2003) – 450,000
9. Woodstock (1969) – 400,000
10. Blockbuster RockFest (21 June 21 1997) – 385,000

TOP TEN LONGEST SONGS

1   'Surgical Sound Specimens From the Museum of Skin' – Fantômas –
    74 min. 17 sec.

2   'Dopesmoker' – Sleep – 63 min. 31 sec.

3   'The Incident' – The Porcupine Tree – 55 min. 8 sec.

4   'Mountain Jam'– Allman Brothers – 44 min.

5   'In Memory of Liz Reed-Georgia on My Mind' – Allman Brothers – 43
    min. 57 sec.

6   'Part 10 Exit Music (The Beginning Stages of...)' – The Polyphonic
    Spree – 36 min. 30 sec.

7   'Performance 2' – John Frusciante – 35 min. 32 sec.

8   'Red Flag (The Secret in Disguise)' Sunburned Hand of the Man – 34
    min. 52 sec.

9   'Zone' – Lightning Bolt – 32 min. 46 sec.

10 'Cassandra Gemini' – The Mars Volta – 32 min. 31 sec.

TOP TEN MOST SUCCESSFUL CONCERT TOURS (BY ATTENDANCE)

1   The Rolling Stones' A Bigger Bang Tour (21–26 August 2007) – 4,680,000

2   U2's Vertigo Tour (28 March to 9 December 2006) – 4,619,021

3   Michael Jackson's HIStory World Tour (7 September 1996 to 15 October 1997) – 4,500,000

4   Michael Jackson's Bad World Tour (12 September 1987 to 27 January 1989) – 4,400,000

5   U2's Popmart Tour, U2 (25 April 25 1997 to 21 March 1998) – 3,935,936

6   Madonna's Sticky & Sweet Tour (23 August 2008 to 2 September 2009) – 3,500,000

7   Cher's Living Proof: The Farewell Tour (14 June 2002 to 30 April 2005) – 3,500,000

8   The Rolling Stones' Licks Tour (3 September 2002 to 9 November 2003) – 3,400,000

9   U2's 360° Tour, U2 (30 June 2009 to 8 October 2010) – 3,071,290 (expected)

10 Tina Turner's Wildest Dreams Tour (20 April 1996 to 10 August 1997) – 3 million

MADONNA'S TOP FIVE MOST SUCCESSFUL STUDIO ALBUMS

	ALBUM TITLE	YEAR OF RELEASE	UNITS SOLD
1	*True Blue*	1986	24 million
2	*Like a Virgin*	1984	21 million
3	*Ray of Light*	1998	20 million
4	*Like a Prayer*	1989	13 million
5	*Confessions on a Dancefloor*	2005	12 million

THE BEATLES' UK OFFICIAL STUDIO ALBUMS

ALBUM TITLE	RELEASE DATE
Please Please Me	22 March 1963
With The Beatles	22 November 1963
A Hard Day's Night	10 July 1964
Beatles For Sale	4 December 1964
Help!	6 August 1965
Rubber Soul	3 December 1965
Revolver	5 August 1966
Sgt Pepper's Lonely Hearts Club Band	1 June 1967
The Beatles aka The White Album	22 November 1968
Yello Submarine	13 January 1969
Abbey Road	26 September 1969
Let It Be	8 May 1970

THE WORLD'S BIGGEST RECORD LABELS*

	RECORD LABEL	REVENUE
1	Universal Music Group	$5.92 billion
2	Sony Music Entertainment	$5.51 billion
3	Warner Music Group	$3.176 billion
4	EMI Group	$1.6 billion

* Information compiled in 2009.

TOP FIVE FASTEST RAPPERS

1. Rebel XD (Seandale Price) – 852 syllables in 42 sec. = 20.29 syllables per sec.

2. Outsider (Shin Ok-cheol) – 18.5 syllables per sec. (in Korean)

3. No Clue (Ricky Brown) – 723 syllables in 41.27 sec. = 17.51 syllables per sec.

4. Chojin (Domingo Edjang Moreno) – 921 syllables in a min. = 15.35 syllables per sec. (in Spanish)

5. Tonedeff (Tony Rojas) – 13.5 syllables per sec.

TOP TEN MOST EXPENSIVE MUSIC VIDEOS

	SONG TITLE	ARTIST	PRODUCTION COST
1	'Scream'	Michael Jackson and Janet Jackson	$7 million
2	'Die Another Day'	Madonna	$6.1 million+
3	'Express Yourself'	Madonna	$5 million+
4	'Bedtime Story'	Madonna	$5 million+
5	'Estranged'	Guns N' Roses	$4 million
6	'Victory'	Puff Daddy (feat. Notorious B.I.G. and Busta Rhymes)	$2.7 million+
7	'Too Legit to Quit'	MC Hammer	$2.5 million+
8	'Heartbreaker'	Mariah Carey feat. Jay-Z	$2.5 million
9	'What's It Gonna Be?!'	Busta Rhymes (feat. Janet Jackson)	$2.4 million+
10	'It's All Coming Back to Me Now'	Celine Dion	$2.3 million+

TOP TEN LOUDEST BANDS

1   Sleazy Joe – **143.2 dB** in 2008. Recorded in Hässleholm, Sweden

2   Swans – **140 dB** – 1985 in London

3   Manowar – **139 dB** in 2008 at the Magic Circle Fest

4   KISS – **136 dB** on 15 July 2009 at the Cisco Ottawa BluesFest in Ottawa, Canada

5   Gallows – **132.5 dB** in 2007. In recording studio

6   My Bloody Valentine – **132 dB**

7   AC/DC – **130 dB**

8   Led Zeppelin – 'Heartbreaker' is said to have reached **130 dB**

9   The Who – **126 dB** show on 31 May 1976 at The Valley (Charlton Athletic FC)

10 Iron Maiden – **124 dB**

FASCINATING FACT

- Ear damage starts at 80 decibels!

TOP TEN ALL TIME BEST-SELLING ALBUMS IN THE UK

ALBUM	ARTIST	UNITS SOLD
1 *Greatest Hits: Volume One*	Queen	5.4 million
2 *Sgt Pepper's Lonely Hearts Club Band*	The Beatles	4.8 million
3 *(What's the Story) Morning Glory?*	Oasis	4.3 million
4 *Brothers in Arms*	Dire Straits	4 million
5 *ABBA Gold: Greatest Hits*	ABBA	3.9 million
6 *The Dark Side of the Moon*	Pink Floyd	3.8 million
7 *Greatest Hits: Volume Two*	Queen	3.6 million
8 *Thriller*	Michael Jackson	3.6 million
9 *Bad*	Michael Jackson	3.6 million
10 *The Immaculate Collection*	Madonna	3.4 million

THE ORCHESTRA

The typical symphony orchestra consists of four proportionate groups of similar musical instruments. See examples below:

SECTION	INSTRUMENTS
Woodwinds	piccolo, flute, oboe, English horn, clarinet, bass clarinet, bassoon, contrabassoon
Brass	french horn, trumpet, trombone, bass trombone, tuba
Percussion	timpani, snare drum, bass drum, cymbals, triangle, celesta
Strings	harp, violin, viola, cello, double bass

- Domenico Dragonetti (1763-1846) was the first great virtuoso of the double bass; he was largely responsible for its permanent place in the orchestra.

- The clarinet's predecessor was the chalumeau, the first true single reed instrument.

- The name dulcimer comes from the Latin and Greek works *dulce* and *melos*, which combine to mean 'sweet tune'.

- The ocarina, a musical wind instrument, is also known as the Sweet Potato.

- A piano covers the full spectrum of all orchestra instruments, from below the lowest note of the double bassoon to above the top note of the piccolo. A grand piano can be played faster than an upright (spinet) piano.

- Guitar probably comes from the word *kithara*, which was the principal stringed instrument of the ancient Greeks and later of the Romans. The *kithara* was played with a plectrum and it was a larger and stronger form of the lyre.

THE TOP SELLING SINGLES OF ALL TIME

1   'Candle in the Wind '97', Elton John - 33 million

2   'White Christmas' Bing Crosby – 30 million

3   'Rock Around the Clock' Bill Haley – 25 million

MUSICAL FIRSTS

- In the 1820s, Louis Spohr introduced the conductor's baton.
- The CD was developed by Philips and Sony in 1980.
- The LP (long-playing) record was invented by Paul Goldmark in 1948.
- At the first Grammy Awards, held on 4 May 1959, Domenico Modugno won the 'Record of the Year', with *Volare*.
- The first pop video was 'Bohemian Rhapsody' by Queen, released in 1975.
- In 1987, Queen of Soul, Aretha Franklin, was the first female artist to be inducted into the Rock 'n' Roll Hall of Fame, followed by The Supremes in 1988.
- Beethoven was the first composer who never had an official court position, thus the first known freelance musician.
- The first ever number one when the charts began in 1952 was Al Martino's 'Here in My Heart'.
- In 1473, just a few decades after the invention of the printing press by Johannes Gutenberg, the first mechanically printed music, the 'Constance Gradual', was published in southern Germany.

 # MUSICAL MOSTS

- Annie Lennox holds the record for the most Brit awards (8).
- The harmonica is the world's best-selling music instrument.
- More than 2,500 cover versions of The Beatles' 'Yesterday' exist, making it the most recorded song in history.
- The British (per capita) spend the most on pre-recorded music.

MOZART'S MILESTONES

1756	Born in Salzburg, Austria, on January 27
1762	Embarked with his father and sister on the first of many concert tours through Europe
1769	Became honorary concertmaster to the Archbishop of Salzburg, a position he retained until 1781
1770	Produced the opera *Mithridates*, King of Pontus
1770	Was made a chevalier of the 'Order of the Golden Spur' by Pope Clement XIV
1781	The opera *Idomeneo, King of Crete* was first performed
1781	Left his post in Salzburg and spent the last years of his life working in Vienna as a composer and teacher
1786	The opera *The Marriage of Figaro* was first performed
1787	The opera *Don Giovanni* was first performed
1790	The opera *Così fan Tutte* was first performed
1791	Composed *The Magic Flute*. Died on 5 December and laid to rest in an unmarked grave

MUSICAL INSTRUCTIONS

SPEED

INSTRUCTION	MEANING
Largo	Very slow
Lento	Slowly
Adagio	Slow
Andante	Walking pace
Moderato	Moderately

Allegro	Quick and lively
Molto allegro	Very fast
Presto	Very quickly
Prestissimo	As fast as possible
Rallentando	Slowing down
Accelerando	Speeding up

CHARACTER

INSTRUCTION	MEANING
Con brio	With vigour
Dolce	Sweetly
Doloroso	Sadly
Giocoso	Merrily
Leggiero	Lightly
Pesante	Heavily
Maestoso	Majestically
Scherzando	Jokingly playfully
Vivace	Lively

SOUND

INSTRUCTION	MEANING
Pianissimo	Very soft
Piano	Soft
Mezzo piano	Medium soft
Mezzo forte	Medium loud
Forte	Loud
Fortissimo	Very loud
Diminuendo	Getting softer
Crescendo	Getting louder

(INSTRUCTION)	(MEANING)
Attacca	Continue without break
Da Capo	Return to beginning
Arco	Bowed
Pizzicato	Plucked
Glissando	Slide
Legato	Smoothly
Staccato	Detached
Volta Subito	Turn page quickly
Fine	End
Con	With
Senza	Without
Molto	Very
Poco	A little

THE NATURAL WORLD

TOP TEN WORLD'S LARGEST DESERTS

	DESERT	COUNTRY	SIZE
1	Sahara	North Africa	3.5 million sq miles (9 million sq km)
2	Gobi	Mongolia/China	500,000 sq miles (1.3 million sq km)
3	Arabian	Egypt	385,000 sq miles (1 million sq km)
4	Kalahari	Botswana/Namibia/South Africa	220,000 sq miles (570,000 sq km)
5	Great Victoria	Australia	135,000 sq miles (350,000 sq km)
6	Taklimakan Shamo	Mongolia/China	125,000 sq miles (320,000 sq km)
7	Kara Kum	Turkmenistan	120,000 sq miles (310,000 sq km)
8	Great Sandy	Australia	100,000 sq miles (260,000 sq km)
9	Thar	India/Pakistan	100,000 sq miles (260,000 sq km)
10	Somali Desert	Somalia	100,000 sq miles (260,000 sq km)

TOP FIVE WORLD'S MOST POPULOUS CITIES ON EARTHQUAKE FAULT LINES

1	Tokyo	4	Mumbai
2	Mexico City	5	Delhi
3	New York		

TOP TEN WORLD'S HOTTEST PLACES

	PLACE	COUNTRY	HIGHEST RECORDED TEMP.
1	Al'Aziziyah	Libya	58°C (136.4°F)
2	Greenland Ranch	Nevada, USA	56.6°C (134°F)
3	Ghudamis	Libya	55°C (131°F)
4	Kebili	Tunisia	55°C (131°F)
5	Tombouctou	Mali	54.5°C (130.1°F)
6	Araouane	Mali	54.4°C (130°F)
7	Tirat Tavi	Israel	53.8°C (129°F)
8	Ahwaz	Iran	53.5°C (128.3°F)
9	Agha Jari	Iran	53.3 °C (128°F)
10	Wadi Halfa	Sudan	52.7°C (127°F)

TOP TEN WORLD'S COLDEST PLACES

	PLACE	COUNTRY	LOWEST RECORDED TEMP.
1	Vostok	Antarctica	-89.2 °C (-138.6 °F)
2	Plateau Station	Antarctic	-84°C (-129.2°F)
3	Oymyakon	Russia	-71.1 °C (-96°F)
4	Verkhoyansk	Russia	-67.7 °C (-90°F)
5	Northice	Greenland	-66°C (-87°F)
6	Eismitte	Greenland	-64.9 °C (-85°F)
7	Snag	Yukon, Canada	-63°C (-81.4°F)
8	Prospect Creek	Alaska, USA	-62.1°C (-79.8°F)
9	Fort Selkirk	Yukon, Canada	-58.9 °C (-74°F)
10	Rogers Pass	Montana, USA	-56.5 °C (-69.7°F)

TOP TEN WORLD'S LONGEST MOUNTAIN RANGES

	MOUNTAIN RANGE	COUNTRY	SIZE
1	Cordillera de Los Andes	South America	4,500 miles (7,200 km)
2	Rocky Mountains	North America	3,000 miles (4,800 km)
3	Himalaya-Karakoram-Hindu Kush	Central Asia	2,400 miles (3,850 km)
4	Great Dividing Range	Australia	2,250 miles (3,620 km)
5	Trans-Antarctic Mountains	Antarctica	2,200 miles (3,540 km)
6	Atlantic Coast Range	Brazil	1,900 miles (3,050 km)
7	West Sumatran-Javan Range	Indonesia	1,800 miles (2,900 km)
8	Aleutian Range	Alaska and NW Pacific	1,650 miles (2,650 km)
9	Tien Shan	Central Asia	1,400 miles (2,250 km)
10	Central New Guinea Range	Papua New Guinea	1,250 miles (2,010 km)

TOP TEN WORLD'S LARGEST LAKES

	LAKE	COUNTRY	SIZE
1	Caspian Sea	Iran/Azerbaijan/ Russia/Turkmenistan/ Kazakhstan	143,000 sq miles (371,000 sq km)
2	Michigan-Huron	USA/Canada	45,300 sq miles (117,610 sq km)
3	Superior	USA/Canada	31,700 sq miles (82,100 sq km)
4	Victoria	Uganda/Tanzania/Kenya	26,828 sq miles (69,500 sq km)
5	Tanganyika	Dem. Rep. of Congo/ Tanzania/Zambia/ Burundi	12,665 sq miles (32,900 sq km)
6	Great Bear	Canada	12,096 sq miles (31,328 sq km)
7	Baykal (Baikal)	Russia	11,776 sq miles (30,500 sq km)
8	Malawi (Nyasa)	Tanzania/Malawi/ Mozambique	11,150 sq miles (28,900 sq km)
9	Great Slave	Canada	11,031 sq miles (28,570 sq km)
10	Erie	USA/Canada	9,910 sq miles (25,670 sq km)

TOP TEN WORLD'S DEEPEST LAKES

	LAKE	COUNTRY	SIZE
1	Baikal	Russia	1,637 m (5,371 ft)
2	Tanganyika	Burundi/Tanzania/ Dem. Rep. of Congo/ Zambia	1,470 m (4,825 ft)
3	Caspian Sea	Azerbaijan/Iran/ Kazakhstan/Russia/ Turkmenistan	1,025 m (3,363 ft)
4	Malawi	Malawi/Mozambique/ Tanzania	706 m (2,316 ft)
5	Issyk Kul	Kyrgyzstan	702 m (2,303 ft)
6	Great Slave	Canada	614 m (2,015 ft)
7	Danau Toba	Indonesia	590 m (1,936 ft)
8	Hornindalsvastnet	Norway	514 m (1,686 ft)
9	Sarezskoye Ozero	Tajikistan	505 m (1,657 ft)
10	Tahoe	USA	501 m (1,645 ft)

TEN OF THE WORLD'S BIGGEST RECORDED EARTHQUAKES

	PLACE	DATE	RICHTER MAGNITUDE
1	Chile (offshore)	22 May 1960	9.5
2	Prince William Sound	Alaska, 28 March 1964	9.2
3	Northern Sumatra (offshore)	Indonesia, 26 December 2004	9.1
4	Kamchatka	Russia, 11 April 1952	9.0
5	Chile (offshore)	27 February 2010	8.8
6	Ecuador (offshore)	31 January 1906	8.8
7	Rat Islands	Alaska, 4 February 1965	8.7
8	Northern Sumatra (offshore)	Indonesia, 28 March 2005	8.6
9	Assam	Tibet, 15 August 1950	8.6
10	Andreanof Islands	Alaska, 9 March 1957	8.6

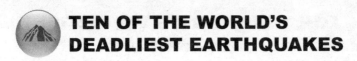

TEN OF THE WORLD'S DEADLIEST EARTHQUAKES

	PLACE	DATE	NUMBER OF FATALITIES
1	Shaanxi Province, China	23 January 1556	830,000
2	Tangshan, China	28 July 1976	242,000
3	Aleppo, Syria	9 August 1138	230,000
4	Haiti	12 January 2010	222,517
5	Xining, China	22 May 1927	200,000
6	Damghan, Iran	22 December 1856	200,000
7	Gansu, China	16 December 1920	200,000
8	Ardabil, Iran	23 March 1893	150,000
9	Kwanto, Japan	1 September 1923	143,000
10	Ashgabat, Turkmenistan, USSR	5 October 1948	110,000

TOP TEN WORLD'S HIGHEST ACTIVE VOLCANOES

VOLCANO	COUNTRY	HEIGHT ABOVE SEA LEVEL
1 Volcan Llullaillaco	Andes, Argentina/Chile	6,723 m (22,057 ft)
2 Volcan Guallatiri	Andes, Chile	6,069 m (19,882 ft)
3 Cotopaxi	Andes, Ecuador	5,897 m (19,347 ft)
4 Tupungatito	Andes, Chile	5,640 m (18,504 ft)
5 Lascar	Andes, Chile	5,591 m (18,346 ft)
6 Popocatepetl	Mexico	5,465 m (17,930 ft)
7 Nevado de Ruiz	Colombia	5,321 m (17,457 ft)
8 Sangay	Andes, Ecuador	5,188 m (17,021 ft)
9 Irruputuncu	Chile	5,163 m (16,939 ft)
10 Klyuchevskaya Sopka	Russia	4,835 m (15,863 ft)

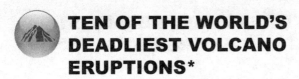

TEN OF THE WORLD'S DEADLIEST VOLCANO ERUPTIONS*

	PLACE	DATE	NUMBER OF FATALITIES
1	Laki, Iceland	1783	2 million
2	Tambora, Indonesia	1815	71,000
3	Krakatoa, Indonesia	1883	37,000
4	Mount Pelee, Martinique	1902	30,000
5	Mount Vesuvius, Pompeii	AD 79	25,000
6	Nevado Del Ruiz, Colombia	1985	23,000
7	Unzen, Japan	1792	15,000
8	Kelut, Java	1919	5,000
9	Papandayan, Java	1772	3,000
10	Mount Lamington, Papua New Guinea	1951	3,000

* All approximate figures.

TEN OF THE WORLD'S MOST DESTRUCTIVE HURRICANES*

	PLACE	DATE	NUMBER OF FATALITIES
1	Bhola Cyclone, Bangladesh	13 November 1970	300-500,000
2	Calcutta Cyclone, Bengal, India	7 October 1737	300,000
3	Haiphong Cyclone, Haiphong, Vietnam	1881	300,000
4	Super Typhoon Nina, China	7 August 1975	210,000
5	Bengal Cyclone, Bengal, India	1876	200,000
6	Cyclone Nargis, Burma	3 May 2008	146,000
7	Bangladesh Cyclone, Bangladesh	29 April 1991	138,800
8	Bombay Cyclone, Bombay, India	6 June 1882	100,000
9	Calcutta, India	5 October 1864	50-70,000
10	Swatow Typhoon, China	1 August 1922	60,000

* Approximate figures, as of 2008.

TEN OF THE WORLD'S DEADLIEST FLOODS

	PLACE	DATE	NUMBER OF FATALITIES
1	Huang He (Yellow) River, China	1931	1 to 3.7 million
2	Huang He River	1887	900,000 to 2 million
3	Huang He River	1938	500,000 to 900,000
4	Kaifeng Flood, China	1642	300,000
5	Ru River, Banqiao Dam, China	1975	230,000
6	Yangtze River, China	1931	145,000
7	The Netherlands and England	1099	100,000
8	The Netherlands	1287	50,000 to 80,000
9	The Neva River, Russia	1824	10,000
10	St Elizabeth's Flood, The Netherlands	1421	10,000

TOP TEN WORLD'S LARGEST SEAS

	SEA	SIZE
1	South China	1,148,500 sq miles (2,974,600 sq km)
2	Caribbean	971,400 sq miles (2,515,900 sq km)
3	Mediterranean	969,100 sq miles (2,509,900 sq km)
4	Bering	873,000 sq miles (2,261,000 sq km)
5	Gulf of Mexico	582,100 sq miles (1,507,600 sq km)
6	Okhotsk	537,500 sq miles (1,392,000 sq km)
7	Japan	391,100 sq miles (1,012,900 sq km)
8	Hudson Bay	281,900 sq miles (730,100 sq km)
9	East China	256,600 sq miles (664,600 sq km)
10	Andaman	218,100 sq miles (564,880 sq km)

TOP TEN WORLD'S DEEPEST SEAS

	SEA	DEPTH
1	Caribbean	8,605 m (28,232 ft)
2	East China (Ryu Kyu Trench)	7,507 m (24,629 ft)
3	South China	7,258 m (23,812 ft)
4	Mediterranean (Ionian Basin)	5,150 m (16,896 ft)
5	Andaman	4,267 m (14,000 ft)
6	Bering	3,936 m (12,913 ft)
7	Gulf of Mexico	3,504 m (11,496 ft)
8	Okhotsk	3,365 m (11,040 ft)
9	Japan	3,053 m (10,016 ft)
10	Red Sea	2,266 m (7,434 ft)

THE WORLD'S OCEANS

OCEAN	SIZE
Pacific	59,270,000 sq miles (155,557,000 sq km)
Atlantic	29,638,000 sq miles (76,762,000 sq km)
Indian	26,467,000 sq miles (68,556,000 sq km)
Southern	7,848,300 sq miles (20,327,000 sq km)
Arctic	5,427,000 sq miles (14,056,000 sq km)

TOP TEN WORLD'S LONGEST CAVES

	CAVE	LENGTH
1	Mammoth Cave, USA	367 miles (590.6 km)
2	Jewel Cave, USA	140 miles (225.4 km)
3	Optimisticheskaya, Ukraine	133 miles (215 km)
4	Wind Cave, USA	128 miles (205.6 km)
5	Lechuguilla Cave, USA	123 miles (198.6 km)
6	Hölloch, Switzerland	121 miles (194.2 km)
7	Fisher Ridge System, USA	110 miles (177.3 km)
8	Sistema Ox Bel Ha (submerged), Mexico	106 miles (169.9 km)
9	Sistema Sac Actun (submerged), Mexico	98 miles (157.3 km)
10	Siebenhengste-Hohgant-Höhle, Switzerland	96 miles (154 km)

TOP TEN DEEPEST DEPRESSIONS ON THE EARTH'S SURFACE

	PLACE	COUNTRY	DEPTH
1	The Dead Sea	Jordan, Israel	408 m (1,338 ft)
2	Lake Assal	The Rep. of Djibouti	156 m (511 ft)
3	Turfan Depression	Sinkiang, China	153 m (505 ft)
4	Qattara Depression	Egypt	132 m (436 ft)
5	Mangyshlak Peninsula	Kazakhstan	131 m (433 ft)
6	Danakil Depression	Ethiopia	116 m (383 ft)
7	Death Valley	California, USA	86 m (282 ft)
8	Salton Sink	California, USA	71 m (235 ft)
9	West of Ustyurt plateau	Kazakhstan	70 m (230 ft)
10	Prikaspiyskaya Nizmennost	Russia Kazakhstan	67 m (220 ft)

* Figures indicate the maximum depth below sea level.

TOP TEN WORLD'S LONGEST RIVERS

1   Nile: Ethiopia, Sudan, Egypt, Uganda, Dem. Rep. of the Congo – 4,160 miles (6,695 km)

2   Amazon: Peru, Colombia, Brazil, Bolivia, Venezuela, Ecuador, Guyana – 3,969 miles (6,387 km)

3   Mississippi: USA – 3,896 miles (6,270 km)

4   Yangtze (Chang Jiang): China – 3,859 miles (6,211 km)

5   Ob-Irtysh: Russia – 3,362 miles (5,410 km)

6   Yenesei: Russia, Mongolia – 3,449 miles (5,550 km)

7   Yellow (Huang He): China – 2,900 miles (4,667 km)

8   Congo: Rep. of Congo, Angola, Zambia, Tanzania, Burundi, Rwanda – 2,716 miles (4,371 km)

9   Amur: Russia, China – 2,714 miles (4,368 km)

10 Lena: Russia – 2,647 miles (4,260 km)

THE LONGEST RIVER IN...

Australia	Murray-Darling – 2,330 miles (3,750 km)
Europe	Danube – 1,771 miles (2,850 km)
France	Loire – 629 miles (1,012 km)
UK	Severn – 220 miles (354 km)
England	Thames – 215 miles (346 km)
Scotland	Tay – 120 miles (193 km)
Wales	Towy – 67 miles (108 km)

TOP TEN WORLD'S HIGHEST MOUNTAINS

	MOUNTAIN	COUNTRY	HEIGHT
1	Mount Everest	Nepal/Tibet	8,848 m (29,029 ft)
2	K2	Pakistan/Sinkiang	8,611 m (28,251 ft)
3	Kangchenjunga	Nepal/India	8,586 m (28,169 ft)
4	Lhotse	Nepal/Tibet	8,516 m (27,940 ft)
5	Makalu	Nepal/Tibet	8,485 m (27,838 ft)
6	Cho Oyu	Nepal/Tibet	8,188 m (26,864 ft)
7	Dhaulagiri	Nepal	8,167 m (26,795 ft)
8	Manaslu	Nepal	8,163 m (26,781 ft)
9	Nanga Parbat	Pakistan	8,125 m (26,657 ft)
10	Annapurna 1	Nepal	8,091 m (26,545 ft)

THE HIGHEST MOUNTAIN IN...

South America	Aconcagua, Argentina – 6,962 m (22,841 ft)
North America	Mount McKinley, Alaska – 6,197 m (4,255 ft)
Africa	Kilimanjaro, Tanzania – 5,895 m (19,341 ft)
Europe	Mount Elbrus, Russia – 5,642 m (18,510 ft)
Australia	Mount Kosciuszko, New South Wales – 2,228 m (7,310 ft)
Scotland	Ben Nevis, Lochaber – 1,344 m (4,409 ft)
Ireland	Carrantuohil, Kerry – 1,039 m (3,409 ft)
Wales	Snowdon, Snowdonia – 1,038 m (3,406 ft)
England	Scafell Pike, Cumbria – 978 m (3,209 ft)

TOP FIVE WORLDS LARGEST ISLANDS

1	Greenland
2	New Guinea
3	Borneo
4	Madagascar
5	Baffin Island

TOP TEN WORLD'S HIGHEST WATERFALLS

	WATERFALL	COUNTRY	HEIGHT
1	Angel Falls	Venezuela	807 m (2,648 ft)
2	Itatinga	Brazil	628 m (2,060 ft)
3	Cuquenan	Guyana	610 m (2,001 ft)
4	Ormeli	Norway	563 m (1,847 ft)
5	Tysse	Norway	533 m (1,749 ft)
6	Pilao	Brazil	524 m (1,719 ft)
7	Ribbon	Brazil	491 m (1,611 ft)
8	Vestre Mardola	Norway	468 m (1,535 ft)
9	Kaieteur	Guyana	457 m (1,499 ft)
10	Cleve-Garth	New Zealand	450 m (1,476 ft)

TOP TEN WORLD'S MOST POLLUTED PLACES

	PLACE	COUNTRY	CAUSE
1	Chernobyl	Ukraine	Radiation. No. affected: approx. 5.5 million
2	Linfen	China	Automobile and industrial emissions. No. affected: 3 million
3	Sukinda	India	Chromite mines and processing. No. affected: 2.6 million
4	Dzerzinsk	Russia	Chemical weapons manufacturing. No. affected: 300,000
5	Sumgayit	Azerbaijan	Organic chemicals, oil and heavy metals. No. affected: 275,000
6	Kabwe	Zambia	Lead mining and processing. No. affected: 255,000
7	Tianying	China	Mining and processing. No. affected: 140,000
8	Norilsk	Russia	Nickel and metal mining processes. No. affected: 134,000
9	Vapi	India	Industrial Estates. No. affected: 71,000
10	La Oroya	Peru	Heavy metal mining and processing. No. affected: 35,000

THE WORLD'S CONTINENTS (BY SIZE)

CONTINENT	SIZE
Asia	17,212,048 sq miles (44,579,000 sq km)
Africa	11,608,161 sq miles (30,065,000 sq km)
North America	9,365,294 sq miles (24,256,000 sq km)
South America	6,879,954 sq miles (17,819,000 sq km)
Antarctica	5,100,023 sq miles (13,209,000 sq km)
Europe	3,837,083 sq miles (9,938,000 sq km)
Australia/Oceania	2,967,967 sq miles (7,687,000 sq km)

CONTINENTS (BY POPULATION)*

Asia	3,879,000,000
Africa	877,500,000
Europe	727,000,000
North America	501,500,000
South America	379,500,000
Australia/Oceania	32,000,000
Antarctica	0

* Compiled in 2006.

TOP TEN HIGHEST TOWNS IN THE WORLD

	TOWN	COUNTRY	HEIGHT
1	Wenzhuan Qinghai-Tibet	China	5,100 m (16,728 ft)*
2	La Rinconada Puno	Peru	5,100 m (16,728 ft)
3	Parinacota Arica-Parinacota	Chile	4,400 m (14,435 ft)
4	Gaite, Lahaul-Spiti district Himachal Pradesh	India	4,400 m (14,435 ft)
5	Dolpa	Nepal	4,360 m (14,301 ft)
6	El Alto La Paz	Bolivia	4,100 m (13,488 ft)
7	Olacapato Salta	Argentina	4,009 m (13,153 ft)
8	Laya Gasa District	Bhutan	3,820 m (12,533 ft)
9	Raíces	Mexico	3,632 m (11,919 ft)
10	Apartaderos Mérida	Venezuela	3,505 m (11,502 ft)

* Highest city in the world according to *The Guinness Book of World Records*.

TOP TEN COUNTRIES WITH THE LONGEST COASTLINES

	COUNTRY	LENGTH OF COASTLINE
1	Canada	151,485 miles (243,791 km)
2	Indonesia	33,999 miles (54,716 km)
3	Russia	23,396 miles (37,652 km)
4	Philippines	22,559 miles (36,305 km)
5	Japan	18,486 miles (29,750 km)
6	Australia	16,007 miles (25,760 km)
7	Norway	13,624 miles (21,926 km)
8	USA	12,380 miles (19,923 km)
9	New Zealand	9,404 miles (15,134 km)
10	China	9,010 miles (14,500 km)

FASCINATING FACT

- The world has an amazing 221,208 miles (356,000 km) of coastline.

TOP TEN MAJOR-IMPACT CRATERS ON EARTH (DIAMETERS)

	PLACE	COUNTRY	DIAMETER
1	Yucatán Peninsula	Chicxulub, Mexico	105 miles (170 km)
2	Manicouagan Reservoir (Lake Manicouagan)	Central Quebec, Canada	62 miles (100 km)
3	Kara-Kul, Tajikistan, aka Qarokul Lake	Pamir Mountains, Tajikistan	28 miles (45 km)
4	Clearwater lakes	Canada	
		West Clearwater Lake	20 miles (32 km)
		East Clearwater Lake	13.7 miles (22 km)
5	Mistastin Lake	Labrador, Canada	17.4 miles (28 km)
6	Gosses Bluff	Australia	15 miles (24 km)
7	Aorounga Impact Crater	Chad	11 miles (17 km)
8	Deep Bay	Canada	8 miles (13 km)
9	Bosumtwi	Ghana	6 miles (10.5 km)
10	Barringer Crater	Arizona, USA	0.75 miles (1.2 km)

PLACES

MOTTOS OF THE 50 STATES OF AMERICA

STATE	MOTTO
Alabama	We Dare Defend Our Rights
Alaska	North to the Future
Arizona	God Enriches
Arkansas	The People Rule
California	I Have Found It
Colorado	Nothing Without Providence
Connecticut	He Who Transplanted Sustains
Delaware	Liberty and Independence
Florida	In God We Trust
Georgia	Wisdom, Justice and Moderation
Hawaii	The Life of the Land is Perpetuated in Righteousness
Idaho	Let it Be Perpetual
Illinois	State Sovereignty, National Union
Indiana	The Crossroads of America
Iowa	Our Liberties We Prize and Our Rights We Will Maintain
Kansas	To the Stars Through Difficulties
Kentucky	United We Stand, Divided We Fall
Louisiana	Union, Justice, and Confidence
Maine	I direct/I lead
Maryland	Manly Deeds, Womanly Words
Massachusetts	By the Sword We Seek Peace, But Peace Only Under Liberty
Michigan	If You Seek a Pleasant Peninsula, Look About You
Minnesota	The Star of the North
Mississippi	By Valor and Arms
Missouri	Let the Welfare of the People Be the Supreme Law
Montana	Gold and Silver

Nebraska	Equality Before the Law
Nevada	All For Our Country
New Hampshire	Live Free or Die
New Jersey	Liberty and Prosperity
New Mexico	It Grows as it Goes
New York	Excelsior (Ever Upward)
North Carolina	To Be, Rather Than to Seem
North Dakota	Liberty and Union, Now and Forever, One and Inseparable
Ohio	With God, All Things Are Possible
Oklahoma	Labor Conquers All Things
Oregon	She Flies With Her Own Wings
Pennsylvania	Virtue, Liberty and Independence
Rhode Island	Hope
South Carolina	While I Breathe, I Hope. Ready in Soul and Resource
South Dakota	Under God the People Rule
Tennessee	Agriculture and Commerce
Texas	Friendship
Utah	Industry
Vermont	Freedom and Unity
Virginia	Thus Always to Tyrants
Washington	By and By
West Virginia	Mountaineers Are Always Free
Wisconsin	Forward
Wyoming	Equal Rights

FASCINATING FACTS

- In Alabama it is illegal to sell peanuts in Lee County after sundown on a Wednesday, and putting salt on a railroad track may be punishable by death.
- In Louisiana, persons could land themselves in jail for up to ten years for stealing an alligator.
- It is illegal to hunt camels in Arizona.
- It is illegal to sell one's own eye in the state of Texas. It is also illegal for one to shoot a buffalo from the second story of a hotel.

TOP TEN WORLD'S MOST POPULOUS NATIONS

	COUNTRY	POPULATION
1	China	1,273 million
2	India	1,029 million
3	USA	278 million
4	Indonesia	228 million
5	Brazil	174 million
6	Russia	146 million
7	Pakistan	145 million
8	Bangladesh	131 million
9	Japan	127 million
10	Nigeria	126 million

TOP TEN WORLD'S LONGEST PLACE NAMES

1 Krung thep mahanakhon bovorn ratanakosin mahintharayutthaya mahadilok pop noparatratchathani burirom udomratchanivetma-hasathan amornpiman avatarnsathit sakkathattiyavisnukarmprasit, Bangkok, Thailand – 167 letters

2 Taumatawhakatangihangakoauauotamateaturipukakapikimaunga-horonukupokaiwhenuakitanatahu, New Zealand – 85 letters*

3 Gorsafawddachaidraigddanheddogleddollônpenrhynareur-draethce-redigion, Gwynedd, North Wales – 67 letters

4 Llanfairpwllgwyngyllgogerychwyrndrobwllllantysiliogogogoch, Gwynedd, North Wales – 58 letters

5 El Pueblo de Nuestra Señora la Reina de los Ángeles de la Porciún-cula (Los Angeles), California – 57 letters

6 Chargoggagoggmanchaugagoggchaubunagungamaug, Massachusetts, USA – 43 letters

7 Lower North Branch Little Southwest Miramichi (A short river in New Brunswick), Canada – 40 letters

8 Villa Real de la Santa Fé de San Francisco de Asis, Santa Fe, New Mexico – 40 letters

9 Te Whakatakanga-o-te-ngarehu-o-te-ahi-a-Tamatea, New Zealand – 38 letters

10 Meallan Liath Coire Mhic Dhubhghaill, Aultanrynie, Highlands, Scotland – 32 letters

* Translation: The place where Tamatea, the man with the big knees, who slid, climbed, and swallowed mountains, known as Land-eater, played on the flute to his loved one.

COUNTRIES WITH THE MOST LAND BORDERS

COUNTRY	NO. OF BORDERS
China	14
Russian Federation	14
Brazil	10
Congo	9
Germany	9
Sudan	9
Austria	8
France	8
Tanzania	8
Turkey	8
Zambia	8

TOP TEN WORLD'S LARGEST COUNTRIES (BY LAND MASS)

	COUNTRY	SIZE
1	Russia	6,592,846 sq miles (17,075,400 sq km)
2	Canada	3,602,707 sq miles (9,330,970 sq km)
3	China	3,600,947 sq miles (9,326,410 sq km)
4	USA	3,539,242 sq miles (9.166,600 sq km)
5	Brazil	3,265,075 sq miles (8,456,510 sq km)
6	Australia	2,941,283 sq miles (7,617,930 sq km)
7	India	1,147,949 sq miles (2,973,190 sq km)
8	Argentina	1,056,636 sq miles (2,736,690 sq km)
9	Kazakhstan	1,049,150 sq miles (2,717,300 sq km)
10	Sudan	917,374 sq miles (2,376,000 sq km)

TOP TEN WORLD'S SMALLEST COUNTRIES

	COUNTRY	SIZE
1	Vatican City	0.17 sq miles (0.44 sq km)
2	Monaco	0.75 sq miles (1.95 sq km)
3	Nauru	8.2 sq miles (21.2 sq km)
4	Tuvalu	10 sq miles (26 sq km)
5	San Marino	24 sq miles (61 sq km)
6	Liechtenstein	62 sq miles (160 sq km)
7	Marshall Islands	70 sq miles (181 sq km)
8	Seychelles	104 sq miles (270 sq km)
9	Maldives	116 sq miles (300 sq km)
10	St Kitts and Nevis	139 sq miles (360 sq km)

TOP TEN WORLD'S MOST POPULOUS CITIES*

	CITY	COUNTRY	POPULATION
1	Shanghai	China	13.3 million
2	Mumbai (Bombay)	India	12.6 million
3	Buenos Aires	Argentina	11.92 million
4	Moscow	Russia	11.3 million
5	Karachi	Pakistan	10.9 million
6	Delhi	India	10.4 million
7	Manila	Philippines	10.3 million
8	São Paulo	Brazil	10.26 million
9	Seoul	South Korea	10.2 million
10	Istanbul	Turkey	9.6 million

* Numbers shown are the population within the recognised city limits, and do not include people living in the immediate surrounding area outside of the established border of the city.

TOWNS AND THEIR RIVERS IN THE UK

TOWN	RIVER	TOWN	RIVER
Bristol	Avon	Leeds	Aire
Canterbury	Stour	Leicester	Soar
Cardiff	Taff	Limerick	Shannon
Carlisle	Eden	Lincoln	Witham
Colchester	Colne	Liverpool	Mersey
Derby	Derwent	London	Thames
Dublin	Liffey	Maidstone	Medway
Durham	Wear	Manchester	Irwell
Exeter	Exe	Newcastle	Tyne
Glasgow	Clyde	Norwich	Wensum
Gloucester	Severn	Nottingham	Trent
Hereford	Wye	Peterborough	Nene
Hull	Humber	Ripon	Ure
Ipswich	Orwell	Swansea	Tawe
Lancaster	Lune	York	Ouse

COUNTRY CODES FOR CARS

CODE	COUNTRY	CODE	COUNTRY
A	Austria	HR	Croatia
Aus	Australia	I	Italy
B	Belgium	IL	Israel
BG	Bulgaria	IRL	Ireland
C	Cuba	J	Japan
CDN	Canada	JA	Jamaica
CH	Switzerland	MA	Morocco
CS	Czech Republic	MC	Monaco
D	Germany	N	Norway
DK	Denmark	NL	Netherlands
DZ	Algeria	NZ	New Zealand
E	Spain	P	Portugal
EAK	Kenya	PE	Peru
F	France	PL	Poland
GB	Great Britain	PE	Peru
GBA	Alderney	R	Romania
GDG	Guernsey	RA	Argentina
GBJ	Jersey	RC	China
GBM	Isle of Man	RUS	Russia
GBZ	Gibraltar	S	Sweden
GR	Greece	SF	Finland
H	Hungary	YU	Yugoslavia
HKZ	Jordan	ZA	South Africa

NATIONAL NEWSPAPERS OF EUROPE

NEWSPAPER	COUNTRY
ABC	Spain
Algemeen Dagblad/De Telegraaf	The Netherlands
Apogevmatini	Greece
Berlingske Tidende	Denmark
Berliner Zeitung	Germany
Diario de Noticias	Portugal
Il Messaggero	Italy
Irish Times	Ireland
La Stampa	Italy
Le Soir	Belgium
Le Figaro/Le Monde	France
Daily Telegraph/Daily Mail	UK

POLITICS

PARLIAMENTS AROUND THE WORLD

COUNTRY	PARLIAMENT
Denmark	Folketing
France	Assemblée Nationale
Germany	Bundestag and Bundersrat
Iceland	Althing
India	Lok Sabha and Rajya Sabha
Isle of Man	Tynwald
Israel	Knesset
Italy	Senato
Japan	Diet
Netherlands	States-General
Norway	Storting
Portugal	Cortes
Republic of Ireland	Dail
Russia	Duma
Spain	Cortes
Sweden	Riksdag
USA	Congress

POLITICAL SYSTEMS AROUND THE WORLD

COUNTRY	POLITICAL SYSTEM
Australia	parliamentary monarchy
Brazil	presidential republic
Canada	parliamentary monarchy
France	semi-presidential republic
Iran	presidential republic under theocratic tutelage
Ireland	parliamentary republic
India	parliamentary republic
Japan	parliamentary monarchy
Russia	semi-presidential republic
Saudi Arabia	absolute monarchy
Spain	parliamentary monarchy
Thailand	parliamentary monarchy
United Kingdom	parliamentary monarchy
USA	presidential republic

COUNTRIES WITH TWO OR MORE 'CAPITAL' CITIES*

COUNTRY	OFFICIAL CAPITAL	OTHER
Benin	Porto Novo (official capital)	Cotonou (de facto seat of government)
Bolivia	Sucre (official 'constitutional' capital; seat of national judiciary)	La Paz (seat of national administrative and legislative bodies)
Chile	Santiago (official capital; seat of national administrative and judicial bodies)	Valparaís (seat of national legislature)
China	Nanjing (de jure capital)	Taipei ('provisional' and de facto capital due to 1949 Chinese Civil War)
Côte d'Ivoire	Yamoussoukro (official capital)	Abidjan (de facto seat of government)
Malaysia	Kuala Lumpur (official capital; seat of national legislature)	Putrajaya ('administrative centre' and seat of national judiciary)
Montenegro	Podgorica (official and de facto capital)	Cetinje ('old royal capital' historical capital possessing no national governmental functions)
Netherlands	Amsterdam (official 'constitutional' capital)	The Hague ('seat of government', i.e. seat of national administrative, legislative, judicial, and royal bodies)
Philippines	Manila (official and de facto capital, seat of executive and judiciary)	Pasay City (seat of upper legislature)

	Quezon City (seat of lower legislature)	Baguio City (summer capital, seat of executive and judiciary during summer months)
South Africa	Pretoria (administrative capital) Bloemfontein (judicial capital)	Cape Town (legislative capital)
Sri Lanka	Kotte (administrative capital)	Colombo (official commercial capital)
Swaziland	Mbabane (administrative capital)	Lobamba (legislative and royal capital)
Tanzania	Dodoma (official capital)	Dar es Salaam (de facto seat of government)

* The capital city is the principal city associated with the country's government. Sometimes the official capital is not necessarily the seat of government.

PRIME MINISTERS OF BRITAIN SINCE 1900

PRIME MINISTER	PARTY	TERM IN OFFICE
Marquess of Salisbury	Conservative	1895-1902
Arthur Balfour	Conservative	1902-5
Sir Henry Campbell-Bannerman	Liberal	1905-8
Herbert Henry Asquith	Liberal	1916-22
Andrew Bonar Law	Conservative	1922-23
Stanley Baldwin	Conservative	1923, 1924-29, 1935-37
Ramsay MacDonald	Labour	1924, 1929-35
Neville Chamberlain	Conservative	1937-40
Sir Winston Churchill	Conservative	1940-45, 1951-55
Clement Attlee	Labour	1945-51
Sir Anthony Eden	Conservative	1955-57
Harold Macmillan	Conservative	1957-63
Sir Alec Douglas-Home	Conservative	1963-64
Harold Wilson	Labour	1964-70, 1974-76
Edward Heath	Conservative	1970-74
James Callaghan	Labour	1976-79
Margaret Thatcher	Conservative	1979-90
John Major	Conservative	1990-97
Tony Blair	New Labour	1997-2007
Gordon Brown	New Labour	2007-10
David Cameron	Conservative	2010-present

PRESIDENTS OF THE USA SINCE 1900

PRESIDENT	PARTY	TERM IN OFFICE
William McKinley	Republican	1897-1901
Theodore Roosevelt	Republican	1901-09
William H. Taft	Republican	1909-13
Woodrow Wilson	Democrat	1913-21
Warren G. Harding	Republican	1921-23
Calvin Coolidge	Republican	1923-29
Herbert Hoover	Republican	1929-33
Franklin D. Roosevelt	Democrat	1933-45
Harry S. Truman	Democrat	1945-53
Dwight D. Eisenhower	Republican	1953-61
John F. Kennedy	Democrat	1961-63
Lyndon B. Johnson	Democrat	1963-69
Richard M. Nixon	Republican	1969-74
Gerald R. Ford	Republican	1974-77
Jimmy Carter	Democrat	1977-81
Ronald Reagan	Republican	1981-89
George Bush	Republican	1989-93
Bill Clinton	Democrat	1993-2001
George W. Bush	Republican	2001-09
Barack Obama	Democrat	2009-present

SCIENCE AND MEDICINE

TOP TEN LARGEST HUMAN ORGANS

	ORGAN	AVERAGE WEIGHT
1	Skin	10,886 g
2	Liver	1,560 g
3	Brain	1,263 g
4	Lungs	1090 g
5	Heart	265-315 g
6	Kidneys	290 g
7	Spleen	170 g
8	Pancreas	98 g
9	Thyroid	35 g
10	Prostate	20 g

TOP TEN LONGEST BONES

	BONE	AVERAGE LENGTH
1	Femur	50.5 cm
2	Tibia	43.03 cm
3	Fibula	40.5 cm
4	Humerus	36.46 cm
5	Ulna	28.2 cm
6	Radius	26.42 cm
7	7th rib	24 cm
8	8th rib	23 cm
9	Innominate bone or hip bone	18.5 cm
10	Sternum	17 cm

BIG NAMES IN THE SCIENTIFIC AND MEDICAL FIELDS

NAME	ACHIEVEMENTS
Archimedes (287-212 BC)	Greek, discovered areas and theories in mathematics that were being developed two millennia later, founded science of hydrostatics.
Aristotle (384-322 BC)	Greek, one of the most influential figures in the history of Western thought and scientific tradition.
Barnard, Christian (1922-2001)	South African surgeon, he performed first successful heart transplant in December 1967 at Groote Schuur Hospital, South Africa.
Bohr, Niels (1885-1962)	Danish physicist, he furthered atomic physics, Nobel prize for physics in 1922 and assisted in atom bomb research during World War One.
Boyle, Robert (1627-91)	Irish physicist and chemist, Boyle's law in 1662, states that the and volume of gas are inversely proportional at constant temperature.
Copernicus, Nicolaus (1473-1543)	Polish astronomer, published the unpopular theory in 1543 that the sun is at the centre of the universe.
Curie, Marie (1867-1934)	Polish/French physicist, worked on magnetism and radioactivity isolating radium and polonium.
Darwin, Charles (1809-82)	English naturalist, he made many geological and zoological discoveries culminating in his theory of evolution, which he published in 1859.
Davy, Humphrey (1778-1829)	English chemist, discovered the anaesthetic effect of laughing gas, discovered the new metals, potassium, sodium, barium, strontium, calcium and magnesium. Devised safety lamps for miners and was important in promoting science with industry.
Einstein, Albert (1879-1955)	German/Swiss/American mathematical physicist, achieved world fame through his special and general theories of relativity.

Fleming, Alexander (1881-1955)	Scottish bacteriologist, first to use anti-typhoid vaccines on humans and pioneered the use of salvarsan to treat syphilis and in 1928 discovered penicillin by chance.
Galileo (1564-1642)	Italian astronomer, mathematician and natural philosopher, deduced the value of a pendulum for exact measurement of time, proved that all falling bodies, great or small, descend due to gravity at the same rate. He perfected the refracting telescope and was convinced by the Copernican theory, which led to his imprisonment.
Harvey, William (1578-1657)	English physician, discovered the circulation of blood.
Newton, Isaac (1642-1727)	English scientist and mathematician, formulated complete theory of gravitation by 1684, also carried out important work in optics.
Pasteur, Louis (1822-95)	French chemist, father of modern bacteriology and introduced pasteurisation.
Pavlov, Petrovich (1849-1936)	Russian physiologist, studied physiology of circulation, digestion and 'conditioned' or acquired reflexes.
Röntgen, Wilhelm (1845-1923)	German physicist, discovered the electromagnetic rays which he called X-rays in 1895.
Schrödinger, Erwin (1887-1961)	Austrian physicist, originated the study of wave mechanics as part of the quantum theory with the celebrated Schrödinger wave equation.
Thomson, Joseph (1856-1940)	English physicist, studied gaseous conductors of electricity and the nature of cathode rays which led to his discovery of the electron. He also discovered the existence of isotopes of elements.
Volta, Alessandro (1745-1827)	Italian physicist, developed the theory of current electricity, invented an electric battery and discovered the electric composition of water. The electrical 'volt' is named after him.
Watt, James (1736-1819)	Scottish engineer and inventor, developed and improved early models of the steam engine; the watt, a unit of power is named after him and the term horsepower was first used by him.

GREAT MEDICAL DISCOVERIES

DISCOVERY	SCIENTIST	YEAR
Anaesthetic (chloroform)	James Young Simpson	1847
Anaesthetic (ether)	William Morton	1846
Antiseptic surgery	Joseph Lister	1865
Aspirin	Hermann Dreser/Felix Hoffman	1899
Atrophine	Rudolph Brondes	1819
Bacteria	Anton Van Leeuwenhoek	1674
Circulation of the blood	William Harvey	1628
Digitalis	William Withering	1785
Diptheria bacillus	Edwin Klebs	1884
HIV virus identified	Luc Montagnier	1983
Insulin (treatment for diabetes)	Frederick Banting/Charles Best	1922
Morphine	Friedrich Sertürner	1805
Pasteurisation	Louis Pasteur	1861
Penicillin	Alexander Fleming	1928
Rabies vaccine	Louis Pasteur	1885
Salvarsan (bacterial agent)	Paul Ehrlich	1910
Tuberculosis bacillus	Robert Koch	1882
Vaccination (against smallpox)	Edward Jenner	1796
Viruses	Martinus Beirjerinck	1897
Whooping cough bacillus	Jules Bordet	1906
X-rays	Wilhelm Röntgen	1895

THE PH SYSTEM

The pH system was invented in 1909 by Danish chemist Søren Sørensen, and involves the measurement of the concentration of hydrogen ions. In turn this tells us how acidic or alkaline a substance is – pH testing is traditionally performed using litmus paper.

SUBSTANCE	PH LISTING
Hydrochloric acid	0
Car battery acid	1.0
Digestive juices	1-3
Lime juice	2.3
Vinegar	3.0
Orange juice	3.7
Normal rainfall	5.6
Saliva	6.4-6.9
Milk	6.6
Pure water	7.0
Human blood	7.4
Sea water	7.8-8.3

HIGHEST MELTING POINTS

SUBSTANCE	TEMP. IN °C	TEMP. IN °F
Carbon	3,527°C	6,381°F
Tungsten	3,422°C	6,192°F
Rhenium	3,186°C	5,767°F
Osmium	3,033°C	5,491°F
Tantalum	3,017°C	5,463°F

DECIPHERING THE DOCTOR'S NOTES...

DIAGNOSIS	DESCRIPTION
Anaemia	lack of red blood corpuscles
Anosma	loss of sense of smell
Appendicitis	inflammation of the appendix
Arthritis	inflammation of a joint
Astigmatism	eye defect affecting focusing
Aural	of the ear
Brachial	of the arm
Bronchitis	inflammation of the lining of the bronchial tubes
Buccal	of the cheek, mouth
Bursitis	inflammation of a bursa (tennis elbow)
Cardiac	of the heart
Cerebral	of the brain
Cholecystitis	inflammation of the gall bladder
Claudication	lameness
Colitis	inflammation of the colon
Conjunctivitis	inflammation of the conjunctiva
Cranial	of the skull
Cystitis	inflammation of the bladder
Daltonism	colour blindness
Dermatitis	inflammation of the skin
Digital	of the fingers
Diplopia	double vision
Dyspepsia	indigestion
Encephalitis	inflammation of the brain
Epistaxis	nose bleed
Erythrocytes	red blood corpuscles
Fibrositis	inflammation of the fibrous tissue

Genal	of the cheeks
Genial	of the chin
Gingivitis	inflammation of the gums
Glossitis	inflammation of the tongue
Haematic	of the blood
Hemicrania	migraine
Hepatic	of the liver
Hepatitis	inflammation of the liver
Herpes Zoster	shingles
Hypermetropia	long-sightedness
Infectious mononucleosis	glandular fever
Keratitis	inflammation of the cornea
Laryngitis	inflammation of the larynx
Leucocytes	white blood corpuscles
Mastitis	inflammation of the mammary gland
Meningitis	inflammation of the membranes surrounding the brain
Metopic	of the forehead
Myopia	short-sightedness
Nasal	of the nose
Nephritis	inflammation of the kidney
Neuritis	inflammation of the nerves
Occipital	of the back of the head
Opthalmic	of the eye
Oral	of the mouth
Osteitis	inflammation of a bone
Otitis	inflammation of the ear
Parotitis	mumps
Pectoral	of the chest
Pedal	of the foot
Peritonitis	inflammation of the peritoneum
Pertussis	whooping cough

Phagocytes	white blood cells that fight disease by engulfing bacteria
Pharyngitis	inflammation of the mucous membrane of the pharynx
Phlebitis	inflammation of a vein
Pollenosis	hay fever
Pulmonary	of the lungs
Renal	of the kidneys
Rhinitis	inflammation of the mucous membrane of the nose
Rubella	German measels
Scarlatina	scarlet fever
Spondylitis	inflammation of a vertebra
Sternutation	sneezing
Stomatitis	inflammation of the mucous membrane of the mouth
Strabismus	squint
Syncope	fainting
Tarsal	of the ankle
Tonsillitis	inflammation of the tonsils
Traulism	a stammer
Varicella	chicken pox
Volar	of the palm of the hand, sole of the foot

 # THE HUMAN BODY IN NUMBERS

206 – bones in adult human
33 – vertebrae
27 – bones in the hand
26 – bones in the foot
24 – ribs (12 sets)

I'VE BROKEN MY...

MEDICAL NAME	COMMON NAME
Cranium	skull
Malar/Zygomatic bone	cheek
Maxilla	upper jaw
Mandible	lower jaw
Clavicle	collar bone
Scapula	shoulder blade
Sternum	breast bone
Humerus	upper arm
Radius	lower arm
Ulna	lower arm
Carpus	wrist
Metacarpus	hand
Pollex	thumb
Phalanges	fingers, toes
Ilium	hip
Femur	thigh bone (longest bone in body)
Patella	kneecap
Tibia	shin
Fibula	back of leg
Talus	ankle
Metatarsus	foot

SCIENTIFIC DISCOVERIES OF THE TWENTIETH AND TWENTY-FIRST CENTURIES

- Ernest Rutherford was the first man to split the atom in 1917.
- In 1934 Enrico Fermi and collaborators discovered that bombarding uranium with neutrons leads to the production of new radioactive material and a potential new source of energy.
- In 2001 the first draft of the human genome was completed.
- In May 2010 J. Craig Venter Institute created the world's first self-replicating, synthetic bacterial cell proving, in principle, that genomes can be designed by computer and chemically made in a laboratory. This could lead to the design of bacterial cells that produce medicines and fuels and even absorb greenhouse gases.
- In 2007, scientists learned how to reprogramme skin cells into stem cells, without cloning or destroying embryos.

CHEMICAL ELEMENTS

CHEMICAL SYMBOL	SUBSTANCE	CHEMICAL SYMBOL	SUBSTANCE
Ag	Silver	Co	Cobalt
Al	Aluminium	Cr	Chromium
Ar	Argon	Cu	Copper
As	Arsenic	F	Fluorine
Au	Gold	Fe	Iron
B	Boron	H	Hydrogen
Ba	Barium	He	Helium
Br	Bromine	Hg	Mercury
C	Carbon	I	Iodine
Ca	Calcium	K	Potassium
Cl	Chlorine	Kr	Krypton

CHEMICAL SYMBOL	SUBSTANCE	CHEMICAL SYMBOL	SUBSTANCE
Li	Lithium	Ra	Radium
Mg	Magnesium	Rn	Radon
Mn	Manganese	S	Sulphur
N	Nitrogen	Sb	Antimony
Na	Sodium	Si	Silicon
Ne	Neon	Sn	Tin
Ni	Nickel	Sr	Strontium
O	Oxygen	U	Uranium
Os	Osmium	W	Tungsten
P	Phosphorus	Xe	Xenon
Pb	Lead	Zn	Zinc
Pt	Platinum	Zr	Zirconium
Pu	Plutonium		

FASCINATING FACTS

- Osmium is the heaviest element, weighing in at 22.61 g/cm^3. It was discovered in 1803 and one of its uses is for the nibs of fountain pens.

- One kilogram of plutonium would produce an explosion equivalent to 20,000 tons of TNT.

- The half-life of uranium-238 (the most common isotope) is 4.46 billion years, roughly on par with the age of the Earth.

SPACE AND ASTRONOMY

TOP TEN FAMOUS COMETS THROUGHOUT HISTORY

1   Halley's Comet – first observed in 1682 – orbits Earth every 75 to 76 years.

2   Shoemaker Levy-9 – destroyed in 1994 – size unknown (one fragment was 1.2 miles long). Erratic orbit of Jupiter lasts two years.

3   Hyakutake – sighted in March 1996 – approx. 350 million miles long (570 million km). Orbit lasts approx. 100,000 years.

4   Hale Bopp – first observed in 1995 – nucleus has a diameter of 24 miles (40 km). Orbit lasts approx. 2,500 years.

5   Comet Borrelly – first observed in 1904 – nucleus is 5 miles long (8 km).

6   Comet Encke – first observed in 1819 – nucleus has a diameter of 3 miles (4.8 km). Orbit lasts three years.

7   Tempel-Tuttel – first observed in 1865 – is approx. 3.1 miles (5 km) in diameter.

8   Comet Tempel 1 – first observed in 1867 – is approx. 3.7 miles long (6 km). Orbit lasts six years.

9   Comet Wild 2 – first observed in 1978 – is approx. 3.1 miles (5 km) in diameter. An orbit lasts six years.

10 Churyumov-Gerasimenko – thought to be around five kilometres across and currently orbits the sun about every six years.

FASCINATING FACTS

- Shoemaker Levy-9 was destroyed when it collided with Jupiter, breaking into 21 pieces. Just one of these fragments generated an explosion equivalent to 6 million megatonnes of TNT.
- Comet Borrelly is shaped like a giant bowling pin.

MEN ON THE MOON BY MISSION

SHUTTLE MISSION	DATE	ASTRONAUTS
Apollo 11	20 July 1969	Neil Armstrong, Buzz Aldrin
Apollo 12	19 November 1969	Charles Conrad, Alan Bean
Apollo 14	5 February 1971	Alan Shepard, Edgar Mitchell
Apollo 15	30 July 1971	James Irwin, David Scott
Apollo 16	21 April 1972	Charles Duke, John Young
Apollo 17	11 December 1972	Harrison Schmitt, Eugene Cernan

FASCINATING FACTS

- A 'blue moon' is the second of two full moons that fall in the same month. This can occur because full moons occur roughly every 29.5 days, so a blue moon occurs roughly every two and three-quarter years.
- The largest crater on our moon measures 2,100 km in diameter and is 12 km deep.

SPACE EXPLORATION FIRSTS

First woman in space – Valentina Tereshkova in Vostok 6 for USSR on 16 June 1963

First Brit in space – Helen Sharman in Soyuz TM-12 for RKA agency on 18 May 1991

First monkey in space – Albert II (died on re-impact with Earth) in V2 for NASA on 14 June 1949

PLANETS IN ORDER OF PROXIMITY TO THE SUN

PLANET	PROXIMITY TO THE SUN
Mercury	36 million miles
Venus	67 million miles
Earth	93 million miles
Mars	142 million miles
Jupiter	483 million miles
Saturn	886 million miles
Uranus	1,783 million miles
Neptune	2,793 million miles

FASCINATING FACTS

- Pluto was stripped of its planetary status in August 2006. To qualify as a planet, it must orbit around the Sun, be round in shape and have an orbit of its own clear of other planets. Pluto was disqualified because its orbit overlaps with that of Neptune.

- All the planets are named after Greco-Roman gods – for example the largest planet, Jupiter, is named after the king of the gods, and the 'blue planet' Neptune, after the god of the sea.

- Astronomers have found the most Earth-like planet outside our solar system to date, a world which could have water running on its surface. The planet orbits the faint star Gliese 581, which is 20.5 light-years away in the constellation Libra. Scientists say that the benign temperatures on the planet mean any water there could exist in liquid form, and this raises the chances it could also harbour life.

THE SUN IN NUMBERS

½ a billioneth – the amount of the sun's energy which actually reaches Earth.

8 – the time in minutes it takes for light from the sun to reach Earth. If the sun fizzled out, the planet would survive for 8 minutes afterwards.

1,950 – how many times bigger the diameter of the star VY Canis Majoris is than that of the Sun.

149,597,893 – how many kilometres the sun is from Earth.

15 million – how many degrees centigrade the sun measures at its core.

10 billion – the length of the sun's lifetime in years. It is currently middle-aged.

TOP TEN ANNUAL METEOR SHOWERS

	NAME	DATE
1	Quadrantids	1-6 January
2	Lyrids	19-22 April
3	Eta Aquarids	1-8 May
4	Delta Aquarids	15 July to 10 August
5	Perseids	27 July to 17 August
6	Orionids	15-25 October
7	Leonids	14-20 November
8	Andromedids	26 November to 4 December
9	Geminids	9-13 December
10	Ursids	20-22 December

SPORT

TOP FIVE WORLD'S
DEADLIEST SPORTS*

SPORT	NO. OF FATALITIES PER 100,000 PARTICIPANTS IN USA
1	Horse Racing	128
2	Sky Diving	123
3	Hang Gliding	56
4	Mountaineering	51
5	Scuba Diving	11

* Figures represent USA fatalities per 100,000 participants.

FASCINATING FACT

• Did you know that boxing became a legal sport in 1901?

CRICKET WORLD CUP WINNERS

YEAR	COUNTRY		
1975	West Indies	1992	Pakistan
1979	West Indies	1996	Sri Lanka
1983	India	1999	Australia
1987	Australia	2003	Australia
		2007	Australia

FASCINATING FACTS

- Australia's Glenn McGrath has taken the most number of wickets in World Cup cricket history with 71.
- The first international cricket match ever held was between Canada and the USA in September 1844.

TOP TEN CRICKETERS WITH THE MOST CENTURIES IN TEST MATCH CRICKET*

1   Sachin Tendulkar, India: 35 in 132 matches
2   Sunil Gavaskar, India: 34 in 125 matches
3   Steve Waugh, Australia: 32 in 168 matches
4   Brian Lara, West Indies: 31 in 123 matches
5   Ricky Ponting, Australia: 30 in 102 matches
6   Sir Donald Bradman, Australia: 29 in 59 matches
7   Allan Border, Australia: 27 in 156 matches
8   Matthew Hayden, Australia: 26 in 81 matches
9   Sir Garfield Sobers, West Indies: 26 in 93 matches
10 Inzamam-ul-Haq, Pakistan: 25 in 107 matches

* As of February 2010.

TOP TEN FOOTBALLING NATIONS (FIFA RANKING)*

	COUNTRY	FIFA POINTS
1	Spain	1,883
2	Netherlands	1,659
3	Brazil	1,536
4	Germany	1,464
5	Argentina	1,289
6	Uruguay	1,152
7	England	1,125
8	Portugal	1,062
9	Egypt	1,053
10	Chile	988

* Ranked in FIFA points total, as of July 2010.

THE FIFA WORLD CUP IN NUMBERS

3   – The number of winners' medals won by Pelé for Brazil in the years 1958, 1962 and 1970.

3   – The most goals scored in a final by a single player – Geoff Hurst for England vs West Germany in 1966.

5   – The most goals scored in a match – Oleg Salenko for Russia vs Cameroon in 1994.

8   – The number of tournaments in which Scotland haven't advanced from the first round.

11   – The duration in seconds of the fastest goal – scored by Hakan Sukur for Turkey vs South Korea in 2002.

42 years **1** month **8** days   – The age of the oldest world cup player – Roger Milla for Cameroon vs Russia in 1994.

TOP TEN MOST CAPPED FIFA WORLD CUP FINALISTS*

	NAME	COUNTRY	NO. OF CAPS IN WORLD CUP
1	Lothar Matthaus	Germany/West Germany	25
2	Paolo Maldini	Italy	23
3	Diego Maradona	Argentina	21
4	Wladyslaw Zmuda	Poland	21
5	Uwe Seeler	Germany/West Germany	20
6	Grzegorz Lato	Poland	20
7	Cafu	Brazil	20
8	Ronaldo	Brazil	19
9	Wolfgang Overath	West Germany	19
10	Berti Vogts	West Germany	19

* Listed by number of appearances – does not include 2010 World Cup.

TOP TEN MOST CAPPED ENGLAND FOOTBALL PLAYERS*

	NAME	NO. OF CAPS
1	Peter Shilton	125
2	David Beckham	115
3	Bobby Moore	108
4	Bobby Charlton	106
5	Billy Wright	105
6	Bryan Robson	90
7	Michael Owen	89
8	Kenny Sansom	86
9	Gary Neville	85
10	Ray Wilkins	84

* As of June 2010.

MOST CONSECUTIVE MINUTES WITHOUT CONCEDING A FIFA WORLD CUP GOAL

557 – Switzerland: 2 July 1994–21 June 2010
549 – Italy: 17 June 1986–3 July 1990
500 – England: 16 June 1982–3 June 1986

TOP TEN MOST EXPENSIVE FOOTBALL PLAYERS IN TRANSFER FEES

	NAME	TRANSFER	FEE
1	Cristiano Ronaldo	Manchester United to Real Madrid	£80 million (2009)
2	Kaka	AC Milan to Real Madrid	£56 million (2009)
3	Zinedine Zidane	Juventus to Real Madrid	£45.62 million (2001)
4	Luis Figo	Barcelona to Real Madrid	£37 million (2000)
5	Hernan Crespo	Parma to Lazio	£35.5 million (2000)
6	Gianluigi Buffon	Parma to Juventus	£32.6 million (2001)
7	Robinho	Real Madrid to Manchester City	£32.5 million (2008)
8	Christian Vieri	Lazio to Inter Milan	£32 million (1999)
9	Dimitar Berbatov	Tottenham to Manchester United	£30.75 million (2008)
10	Andriy Shevchenko	AC Milan to Chelsea	£30 million (2006)

TOP TEN ENGLAND GOALSCORERS (FOOTBALL)

	NAME	NO. OF GOALS
1	Bobby Charlton (1958-1970)	49 goals (106 caps)
2	Gary Lineker (1984-1992)	48 goals (80 caps)
3	Jimmy Greaves (1959-1967)	44 goals (57 caps)
4	Michael Owen (1998-present)	40 goals (89 caps)
5	Tom Finney (1946-1958)	30 goals (76 caps)
6	Nat Lofthouse (1950-1958)	30 goals (33 caps)
7	Alan Shearer (1992-2000)	30 goals (63 caps)
8	Vivian Woodward (1903-1911)	29 goals (23 caps)
9	Steve Bloomer (1895-1907)	28 goals (23 caps)
10	David Platt (1986-1996)	27 goals (62 caps)

TOP TEN MOST SUCCESSFUL ENGLAND FOOTBALL MANAGERS*

	NAME	SUCCESS RATE
1	Fabio Capello (2008-present)	won 68 per cent of 28 matches
2	Sir Alf Ramsey (1963-1974)	won 61 per cent of 113 matches
3	Glenn Hoddle (1996-1999)	won 61 per cent of 28 matches
4	Ron Greenwood (1977-1982)	won 60 per cent of 55 matches
5	Sven-Göran Eriksson (2001-2006)	won 60 per cent of 10 matches
6	Walter Winterbottom (1946-1962)	won 56 per cent of 28 matches
7	Steve McLaren (2006-2007)	won 50 per cent of 18 matches
8	Sir Bobby Robson (1982-1990)	won 49 per cent of 18 matches
9	Don Revie (1974-1977)	won 48 per cent of 29 matches
10	Terry Venables (1994-1996)	won 48 per cent of 23 matches

* As of June 2010.

TOP TEN WEALTHIEST FOOTBALL CLUBS*

1	Manchester United, England – £1.2 billion
2	Real Madrid, Spain – £873 million
3	Arsenal, England – £780 million
4	FC Barcelona, Spain – £660 million
5	Bayern Munich, Germany – £653 million
6	Liverpool, England – £542 million
7	AC Milan, Italy – £528 million
8	Juventus, Italy – £433 million
9	Chelsea, England – £426 million
10	Internazionale, Italy – £272 million

* As of April 2010.

TOP TEN WEALTHIEST FOOTBALL PLAYERS*

1	Lionel Messi, Argentina, Barcelona – £29.7 million
2	David Beckham, England, LA Galaxy and AC Milan – £27.3 million
3	Cristiano Ronaldo, Portugal, Real Madrid – £27 million
4	Kaka, Brazil, Real Madrid – £16.9 million
5	Thierry Henry, France, Barcelona – £16.2 million
6	Ronaldinho, Brazil, AC Milan – £15.5 million
7	Carlos Tevez, Argentina, Manchester City – £13.8 million
8	Zlatan Ibrahimovic, Sweden, Barcelona – £13 million
9	Frank Lampard, England, Chelsea – £12.8 million
10	Samuel Eto'o, Cameroon, Inter Milan – £12.4 million

* Refers to earnings for 2009.

TOP TEN WEALTHIEST FOOTBALL MANAGERS

1	José Mourinho (Inter Milan) – £10.9 million	
2	Roberto Mancini (Manchester City) – £10.1 million	
3	Felipe Scolari (FC Bunyodkor) – £7.95 million	
4	Jurgen Klinsmann (ex-Bayern Munich) – £7.57 million	
5	Fabio Capello (England) – £7.01 million	
6	Guus Hiddink (Russia) – £6.64 million	
7	Sir Alex Ferguson (Manchester United) – £6.08 million	
8	Pep Guardiola (Barcelona) – £5.43 million	
9	Arsene Wenger (Arsenal) – £5.32 million	
10	Louis Van Gaal (Bayern Munich) – £5.05 million	

*Refers to earnings for 2009.

TOP TEN OLDEST FOOTBALL CLUBS IN UK LEAGUE

	TEAM	YEAR FOUNDED
1	Notts County	1862
2	Stoke City	1863
3	Nottingham Forest	1865
4	Chesterfield	1866
5	Sheffield Wednesday	1867
6	Reading	1871
7	Wrexham	1873
8	Aston Villa	1874
9	Bolton Wanderers	1874
10	Birmingham City	1875

FIFA WORLD CUP GOLDEN BOOT WINNERS

YEAR	NAME	TEAM	NUMBER OF GOALS SCORED
1970	Gerd Mueller	West Germany	10
1974	Grzegorz Lato	Poland	7
1978	Mario Kempes	Argentina	6
1982	Paolo Rossi	Italy	6
1986	Gary Lineker	England	6
1990	Salvatore Schillaci	Italy	6
1994	Oleg Salenko	Russia	6
1998	David Suker	Croatia	6
2002	Ronaldo	Brazil	8
2006	Miroslav Klose	Germany	5
2010	Thomas Müller	Germany	5

FIFA WORLD PLAYER OF THE YEAR WINNERS

YEAR	NAME	TEAM	YEAR	NAME	TEAM
2000	Zidane	France	2005	Ronaldinho	Brazil
2001	Luis Figo	Portugal	2006	Cannavaro	Italy
2002	Ronaldo	Brazil	2007	Kaká	Brazil
2003	Zidane	France	2008	Ronaldo	Portugal
2004	Ronaldinho	Brazil	2009	Messi	Argentina

FIFA WORLD CUP-WINNING NATIONS

COUNTRY	NUMBER OF WINS
Brazil	5
Italy	4
Germany	3
Uruguay	2
Argentina	2
England	1
France	1
Spain	1

TOP TEN LARGEST FOOTBALL STADIUMS BY CAPACITY

	NAME	CAPACITY
1	Rungrado May Day Stadium, Pyongyang, North Korea	150,000
2	Salt Lake Stadium, Kolkata, India	120,000
3	Estadio Azteca, Mexico City, Mexico	105,000
4	Melbourne Cricket Ground, Melbourne, Australia	100,018
5	Bukit Jalil National Stadium, Kuala Lumpur, Malaysia	100,000
6	Camp Nou, Barcelona, Spain	98,772
7	Soccer City, Johannesburg, South Africa	94,700
8	Wembley Stadium, London, UK	90,000
9	Azadi Stadium, Tehran, Iran	90,000
10	Estadio Do Maracana, Rio de Janeiro, Brazil	88,992

TOP TEN FOOTBALL PLAYERS WITH MOST GOALS SCORED IN PREMIER LEAGUE*

NAME	NO. OF GOALS
1 Alan Shearer	260
2 Andrew Cole	187
3 Thierry Henry	174
4 Robbie Fowler	163
5 Les Ferdinand	149
6 Michael Owen	147
7 Teddy Sheringham	147
8 Frank Lampard	129
9 Jimmy Floyd Hasselbaink	127
10 Dwight Yorke	123

* Up to end of season 2009/2010.

TOP TEN MOST APPEARANCES IN THE PREMIER LEAGUE*

1 David James	573	6 Frank Lampard	467
2 Ryan Giggs	548	7 Paul Scholes	443
3 Gary Speed	535	8 Alan Shearer	441
4 Sol Campbell	496	9 Jamie Carragher	435
5 Emile Heskey	469	10 Phil Neville	429

* As of June 2010.

PREMIER LEAGUE FOOTBALL PLAYERS WITH THE MOST RED CARDS*

Richard Dunne	8
Duncan Ferguson	8
Patrick Vieira	8
Vinnie Jones	7
Roy Keane	7
Alan Smith	7
Luis Boa Morte	6
Nicky Butt	6
Eric Cantona	6
Andrew Cole	6

* As of June 2010.

TOP TEN PREMIER LEAGUE CLUB PERFORMERS*

	TEAM	PREMIER LEAGUE POINTS		TEAM	PREMIER LEAGUE POINTS
1	Man Utd	1494	6	Tottenham	955
2	Arsenal	1311	7	Everton	924
3	Chelsea	1267	8	Newcastle	906
4	Liverpool	1224	9	Blackburn	896
5	Aston Villa	1003	10	West Ham	731

* As of June 2010.

F1 IN NUMBERS

1906 – The date that Ferenc Szisz from Romania, driving a Renault, won the first F1 Grand Prix held at Le Mans, France.

375 – The top speed in kilometres per hour of a F1 car.

3,100 – The number of times (on average) a F1 car will change gear during the Monaco Grand Prix.

2 – The number of kilograms (on average) a F1 driver will lose during a grand prix.

1.5 – How many litres of fluid a driver can lose during a hot race.

7 – The number of seconds it takes for an F1 car to go from a standstill to 200 km/h and back again.

46 years **1** month and **11** days – The age of the oldest world champion, Argentina's Juan Manuel Fangio in 1957.

TOP TEN F1 CONSTRUCTOR TEAMS BY CHAMPIONSHIP WINS

	NAME	COUNTRY	WINS
1	Ferrari	Italy	15
2	McLaren	Great Britain	12
3	Williams	Great Britain	7
4	Lotus	Great Britain	6
5	Brabham	Great Britain	4
6	Cooper	Great Britain	2
7	Renault	France	2
8	Benetton	Great Britain	2
9	Mercedes	Germany	2
10	Alfa Romeo	Italy	2

TOP TEN FASTEST WOMEN'S MARATHON TIMES*

	NAME	COUNTRY	MARATHON	TIME
1	Paula Radcliffe	Great Britain	London on 13 Apr. 2003	2:15:25
2	Paula Radcliffe	Great Britain	Chicago on 13 Oct. 2002	2:17:18
3	Paula Radcliffe	Great Britain	London on 17 Apr. 2005	2:17:42
4	Catherine N'dereba	Kenya	Chicago on 7 Oct. 2001	2:18:47
5	Paula Radcliffe	Great Britain	London on 14 Apr. 2002	2:18:56
6	Mizuki Noguchi	Japan	Berlin on 25 Sep. 2005	2:19:12
7	Irina Mikitenko	Germany	Berlin on 28 Sep. 2008	2:19:19
8	Catherine N'dereba	Kenya	Chicago on 13 Oct. 2002	2:19:26
9	Deena Kastor	USA	London on 23 Apr. 2006	2:19:36
10	Yingjie Sun	China	Beijing on 19 Oct. 2003	2:19:39

* As of 14 June 2010.

TOP TEN FASTEST MEN'S MARATHON TIMES*

	NAME	COUNTRY	MARATHON	TIME
1	Haile Gebrselassie	Ethiopia	Berlin on 28 Sep. 2008	2:03:59
2	Haile Gebrselassie	Ethiopia	Berlin on 30 Sep. 2007	2:04:26
3	Duncan Kipkemboi Kibet	Kenya	Rotterdam on 5 Apr. 2009	2:04:27
4	James Kipsang Kwambai	Kenya	Rotterdam on 5 Apr. 2009	2:04:27
5	Patrick Makau	Kenya	Rotterdam on 11 Apr. 2010	2:04:48
6	Haile Gebrselassie	Ethiopia	Dubai on 18 Jan. 2008	2:04:53
7	Paul Tergat	Kenya	Berlin on 28 Sep. 2003	2:04:55
8	Geoffrey Mutai	Kenya	Rotterdam on 11 Apr. 2010	2:04:55
9	Sammy Korir	Kenya	Berlin on 28 Sep. 2003	2:04:56
10	Abel Kirui	Kenya	Rotterdam on 5 Apr. 2009	2:05:04

* As of June 2010.

TOP TEN MOST SUCCESSFUL GOLF PLAYERS*

	NAME	COUNTRY	CAREER	WINS
1	Jack Nicklaus	USA	1962-1986	18
2	Tiger Woods	USA	1997-2008	14
3	Walter Hagen	USA	1914-1929	11
4	Gary Player	South Africa	1959-1978	9
5	Ben Hogan	USA	1946-1953	9
6	Tom Watson	USA	1975-1083	8
7	Arnold Palmer	USA	1958-1964	7
8	Sam Snead	USA	1942-1954	7
9	Gene Sarazen	USA	1922-1935	7
10	Bobby Jones	USA	1923-1930	7

* Based on combined wins of the Masters, the US Open, the Open, and PGA.

TOP TEN PGA RANKED GOLFERS*

	NAME	COUNTRY
1	Tiger Woods	USA
2	Phil Mickelson	USA
3	Lee Westwood	England
4	Steve Stricker	USA
5	Jim Furyk	USA
6	Luke Donald	England
7	Ernie Els	South Africa
8	Ian Poulter	England
9	Paul Casey	England
10	Rory McIlroy	Northern Ireland

* As of June 2010.

- Did you know golf is the only sport to have been played on the moon? On 6 February 1971, astronaut Alan Shepard hit a golf ball.

- The world's oldest golf course, St Andrews in Scotland, was in use as early as the sixteenth century.

 TOP TEN LONGEST UK GOLF COURSES

	PLACE	COUNTRY	YARDS
1	Turnberry Ailsa	Ayrshire, Scotland	7,201
2	Royal County Down	Newcastle, Northern Ireland	7,181
3	Loch Lomond	Dunbartonshire, Scotland	7,140
4	Woodhall Spa Hotchkin	Lincolnshire, England	7,080
5	Muirfield, Gullane	Lothian, Scotland	7,034
6	Carnoustie	Angus, Scotland	6,941
7	Royal Portrush	County Antrim, Ireland	6,867
8	Royal Birkdale	Southport, Merseyside, England	6,817
9	St Andrews Old	Fife, Scotland	6,721
10	Sunningdale Old	Surrey, England	6,627

TOP TEN FASTEST 100 M MALE RUNNERS

	NAME	COUNTRY	TIME
1	Usain Bolt	Jamaica	9.58 sec.
2	Tyson Gay	USA	9.69 sec.
3	Asafa Powell	Jamaica	9.72 sec.
4	Maurice Greene	USA	9.79 sec.
5	Donovan Bailey	Canada	9.84 sec.
6	Bruny Surin	Canada	9.84 sec.
7	Leroy Burrell	USA	9.85 sec.
8	Justin Gatlin	USA	9.85 sec.
9	Olusoji Fasuba	Nigeria	9.85 sec.
10	Carl Lewis	USA	9.86 sec.

TOP TEN FASTEST 100 M FEMALE RUNNERS

	NAME	COUNTRY	TIME
1	Florence Griffith-Joyner	USA	10.49 sec.
2	Carmelita Jeter	USA	10.64 sec.
3	Marion Jones	USA	10.65 sec.
4	Shelly-Ann Fraser	USA	10.73 sec.
5	Christine Arron	France	10.73 sec.
6	Merlene Ottey	Jamaica	10.74 sec.
7	Kerron Stewart	Jamaica	10.75 sec.
8	Evelyn Ashford	USA	10.76 sec.
9	Irina Privalova	Russia	10.77 sec.
10	Ivet Lalova	Bulgaria	10.77 sec.

MOST OLYMPIC MEDALS WON BY AN INDIVIDUAL

	NAME	COUNTRY	SPORT	MEDALS WON
1	Larissa Latynina	Soviet Union	Gymnastics	18
2	Michael Phelps	USA	Swimming	16
3	Nikolai Andrianov	Soviet Union	Gymnastics	15
4	Boris Shakhlin	Soviet Union	Gymnastics	13
5	Edoardo Mangiarotti	Italy	Fencing	13
6	Takashi Ono	Japan	Gymnastics	13

TOP TEN MOST OLYMPIC GOLD MEDALS WON BY AN INDIVIDUAL

	NAME	COUNTRY	SPORT	MEDALS WON
1	Michael Phelps	USA	Swimming	14
2	Larissa Latynina	Soviet Union	Gymnastics	9
3	Paavo Nurmi	Finland	Athletics	9
4	Mark Spitz	USA	Swimming	9
5	Carl Lewis	USA	Athletics	9
6	Bjørn Dæhlie	Norway	Cross-country Skiing	8
7	Birgit Fischer	Germany	Canoeing	8
8	Sawao Kato	Japan	Gymnastics	8
9	Jenny Thompson	USA	Swimming	8
10	Ray Ewry	USA	Athletics	8

TOP TEN MOST OLYMPIC MEDALS WON BY A COUNTRY*

	COUNTRY	MEDALS WON
1	USA	2,549
2	Soviet Union	1,204
3	Great Britain	737
4	France	730
5	Germany	719
6	Italy	627
7	Sweden	604
8	East Germany	519
9	Hungary	465
10	Finland	455

* Figure indicates total number of summer and winter tournament medals.

FASCINATING FACTS

- The first modern Olympic Games were held in Athens, Greece in 1896. There were 311 male, but no female competitors.

- Badminton's Olympic debut was in 1992 in Barcelona. Since 1992, Asian players have won 42 of the 46 Olympic medals. Over 1.1 billion people watched the first Olympic badminton tournament on television.

- The very first Olympic race, held in 776 BC, was won by Corubus, a chef.

- The first Winter Olympics were held in Chamonix, France, in 1924.

- The Olympic flag was first unveiled at Antwerp in 1920, and was finally retired after the 1984 Games at Los Angeles. A new flag was flown at the 1988 Seoul Games. The five rings in the Olympic flag symbolise the five inhabited continents: Europe, Asia, Africa, Australasia and America. It is believed the colours were chosen because at least one of them can be found in the flag of every nation.

TOP TEN MOST CAPPED RUGBY PLAYERS*

	NAME	COUNTRY	CAREER	CAPS
1	George Gregan	Australia	1994-2007	139
2	Jason Leonard	England	1990-2004	119
3	Fabien Pelous	France	1995-2007	118
4	Philippe Sella	France	1982-2005	111
5	George Smith	Australia	2000-2010	110
6	Brian O'Driscoll	Ireland	1999-present	103
7	Gareth Thomas	Wales	1995-2007	103
8	Stephen Larkham	Australia	1996-2007	102
9	Percy Montgomery	South Africa	1997-2008	102
10	Alessandro Troncon	Italy	1994-2007	101

* As of February 2010.

MOST POINTS BY A TEAM IN A SINGLE GAME IN RUGBY WORLD CUP HISTORY

1	25 October 2003: Australia 142 – 0 Namibia
2	4 June 1995: New Zealand 145 – 17 Japan
3	14 October 1999: New Zealand 101 – 3 Italy
4	2 November 2003: England 111 – 13 Uruguay
5	15 September 1995: New Zealand 108 – 13 Portugal
6	26 May 1995: Scotland 89 – 0 Cote D'Ivoire
7	8 September 2007: Australia 91 – 3 Japan
8	18 October 2003: Australia 90 – 8 Romania
9	12 October 2003: England 84 – 6 Georgia
10	29 September 2007: New Zealand 85 – 8 Romania

FIVE MOST RECENT RUGBY WORLD CUP WINNERS

YEAR	COUNTRY
1991	Australia
1995	South Africa
1999	Australia
2003	England
2007	South Africa

MOST POINTS SCORED BY AN INDIVIDUAL IN THE RUGBY WORLD CUP*

	NAME	COUNTRY	POINTS
1	Jonny Wilkinson	England	249
2	Gavin Hastings	Scotland	227
3	Michael Lynagh	Australia	195
4	Grant Fox	New Zealand	170
5	Andrew Mehrtens	New Zealand	163
6	Gonzalo Quesada	Argentina	135
7	Matt Burke	Australia	125
8	Nicky Little	Fiji	125
9	Thierry Lacroix	France	124
10	Gareth Rees	Canada	120

* Includes tries, conversions, penalties and drop goals, as of June 2010.

TEN MOST RECENT 6 NATIONS WINNERS

YEAR	COUNTRY
2001	England
2002	France
2003	England
2004	France
2005	Wales
2006	France
2007	France
2008	Wales
2009	Ireland
2010	France

6 NATIONS WINS

COUNTRY	NUMBER OF WINS
France	5
England	3
Wales	2
Ireland	1
Scotland	0
Italy	0

TOP FOUR TENNIS TOURNAMENTS IN ORDER OF PRIZE MONEY FOR SINGLE PLAYERS*

1	French Open	€5,792,000 (approx. £4.8 million)
2	Australian Open	AU$2.1million (approx. £1.2 million)
3	US Open	$1.7 million (approx. £1.1 million)
4	Wimbledon	£1 million

* In 2010.

TEN MOST RECENT WIMBLEDON CHAMPIONS (MEN'S AND WOMEN'S SINGLES)

YEAR	MEN'S CHAMPION	COUNTRY	WOMEN'S CHAMPION	COUNTRY
2010	Rafael Nadal	Spain	Serena Williams	USA
2009	Roger Federer	Switzerland	Serena Williams	USA
2008	Rafael Nadal	Spain	Venus Williams	USA
2007	Roger Federer	Switzerland	Venus Williams	USA
2006	Roger Federer	Switzerland	Amelie Mauresmo	France
2005	Roger Federer	Switzerland	Venus Williams	USA
2004	Roger Federer	Switzerland	Maria Sharapova	Russia
2003	Roger Federer	Switzerland	Serena Williams	USA
2002	Leyton Hewitt	Australia	Serena Williams	USA
2001	Goran Ivanisevic	Croatia	Venus Williams	USA

TOP FIVE HIGHEST-EARNING MALE TENNIS PLAYERS*

1	Rafael Nadal	$4,024,378 (£2,638,436.41)
2	Roger Federer	$2,701,897 (£1,771,400.06)
3	Robin Soderling	$1,686,908 (£1,105,822.71)
4	Andy Murray	$1,325,947 (£869,201.11)
5	Fernando Verdasco	$1,302,041 (£853,529.95)

* As of July 2010.

TOP FIVE HIGHEST-EARNING FEMALE TENNIS PLAYERS*

1	Serena Williams	$2,644,049 (£1,733,342)
2	Venus Williams	$1,999,788 (£1,310,988.01)
3	Francesca Schiavone	$1,807,361 (£1,184,839.89)
4	Jelena Jankovic	$1,474,451 (£966,613.26)
5	Samantha Stosur	$1,441,567 (£945,055.33)

* As of July 2010.

FASCINATING FACTS

- The first tennis championships for men were held at Wimbledon in 1877 and 22 players competed in the first year.

- In 1884, the first men's doubles and women's singles championships were held at Wimbledon.

- The name 'tennis' comes from the French word *'tenez'*, the imperative form of the verb *'tenir'* (to hold).

- In 1986 yellow balls were used for the first time in Wimbledon to improve visibility.

- The average person will burn 100 calories in just 14 minutes of tennis.

 ## TOP TEN MOST GRAND SLAM WINS – MEN*

1	Roger Federer	16
2	Pete Sampras	14
3	Roy Emerson	12
4	Bjorn Borg	11
5	Rod Laver	11
6	Bill Tilden	10
7	Andre Agassi	8
8	Jimmy Connors	8
9	Ivan Lendl	8
10	Fred Perry	8

* Tournaments include Australian, French Open, US Open and Wimbledon.

TOP TEN MOST GRAND SLAM WINS – WOMEN*

1	Margaret Court	24
2	Steffi Graf	22
3	Helen Wills Moody	19
4	Chris Evert	18
5	Martina Navratilova	18
6	Billie Jean King	12
7	Serena Williams	12
8	Monica Seles	9
9	Maureen Connolly Brinker	9
10	Molla Bjurstedt Mallory	8

* Tournaments include Australian, French Open, US Open and Wimbledon.

TOP FIVE MOST CAREER SINGLES TENNIS TITLES – MEN

1	Jimmy Connors	109
2	Ivan Lendl	94
3	John McEnroe	77
4	Pete Sampras	64
5	Bjorn Borg and Guillermo Vilas	62 (tied)

TOP FIVE MOST CAREER SINGLES TENNIS TITLES – WOMEN

1	Martina Navratilova	167
2	Chris Evert	154
3	Steffi Graf	107
4	Margaret Court	92
5	Billie-Jean King	67

TOP FIVE FASTEST RECORDED FIRST SERVES IN TENNIS

1	Andy Roddick	USA	155 mph (249.4 km/h)
2	Ivo Karlovic	Croatia	153 mph (246 km/h)
3	Taylor Dent	USA	151 mph (243 km/h)
4	Greg Rusedski	Canada	149 mph (240 km/h)
5	Mark Philippoussis	Australia	142.3 mph (229 km/h)

COUNTRIES WITH THE MOST OLYMPIC GOLDS IN DECATHLON

1	USA	12
2	Czech Republic	2
3	Germany	2

COUNTRIES WITH THE MOST
OLYMPIC GOLDS IN BIATHLON*

1	Russia/Soviet Union	16
2	Germany	14
3	Norway	9

* Events in a biathlon are: cross-country skiing and .22 calibre rifle shooting.

TEN MOST RECENT WORLD
SNOOKER CHAMPIONS

YEAR	CHAMPION	COUNTRY
2000	Mark Williams	Wales
2001	Ronnie O'Sullivan	England
2002	Peter Ebdon	England
2003	Mark Williams	Wales
2004	Ronnie O'Sullivan	England
2005	Shaun Murphy	England
2006	Graeme Dott	Scotland
2007	John Higgins	Scotland
2008	Ronnie O'Sullivan	England
2009	John Higgins	Scotland
2010	Neil Robertson	Austrailia

- The fastest frame ever recorded in professional snooker took place on 31 August 1988 when Tony Drago won the fifth frame of his third round Fidelity Unit Trusts International match against Danny Fowler in just three minutes.

- Ronnie O'Sullivan compiled each of the five fastest 147 breaks ever recorded, the fastest of which took five minutes and 20 seconds recorded in the first round of the 1997 World Championship.

TEN MOST RECENT GRAND NATIONAL WINNERS

YEAR	HORSE	JOCKEY	ODDS
2001	Red Marauder	Richard Guest	33/1
2002	Bindaree	Jim Culloty	20/1
2003	Monty's Pass	B.Geraghty	16/1
2004	Amberleigh House	Graham Lee	16/1
2005	Hedgehunter	Ruby Walsh	7/1
2006	Numbersixvalverde	Niall Madden	11/1
2007	Silver Birch	Robbie Power	33/1
2008	Comply or Die	T. Murphy	7/1
2009	Mon Mome	L. Treadwell	100/1
2010	Don't Push It	A. P. McCoy	25/1

FASCINATING FACT

- The most valuable racehorse ever was sold in 2006 at the Calder Racecourse. The colt, descended from two Kentucky Derby winners was bought for $16 million (£10.4 million).

TEN MOST RECENT RECIPIENTS OF THE BBC SPORTS PERSONALITY OF THE YEAR

YEAR	SPORTS STAR	SPORT
2000	Steve Redgrave	Rowing
2001	David Beckham	Football
2002	Paula Radcliffe	Athletics
2003	Jonny Wilkinson	Rugby
2004	Kelly Holmes	Athletics
2005	Andrew Flintoff	Cricket
2006	Zara Phillips	Equestrian
2007	Joe Calzaghe	Boxing
2008	Chris Hoy	Cycling
2009	Ryan Giggs	Football

TOP TEN TEAMS WITH THE MOST SUPERBOWL WINS

1	Pittsburgh Steelers	6
2	San Francisco 49ers	5
3	Dallas Cowboys	5
4	Green Bay Packers	3
5	New York Giants	3
6	Oakland/LA Raiders	3
7	Washington Redskins	3
8	New England Patriots	3
9	Baltimore/Indianapolis Colts	2
10	Miami Dolphins	2

THEATRE

TOP TEN LONGEST-RUNNING MUSICALS IN THE WEST END

1   *Les Misérables*, Barbican/Queen's Theatres – opened 8 October 1985

2   *Phantom of the Opera*, Her Majesty's Theatre – opened 9 October 1986

3   *Blood Brothers*, Albery/Phoenix Theatres – opened 28 July 1988

4   *Cats*, New London Theatre – opened 11 May 1981 and closed 11 May 2002)

5   *Starlight Express*, Apollo Victoria Theatre – opened 27 March 1984 and closed 12 January 2002

6   *Chicago*, Adelphi/Cambridge Theatres – opened 18 November 1997

7   *Buddy – The Buddy Holly Story*, Victoria Palace/Novello Theatres – opened 12 October 1989 and closed 19 May 2002

8   *Mamma Mia!*, Prince Edward/Prince of Wales Theatres – opened 6 April 1999

9   *The Lion King*, Lyceum Theatre – opened 19 October 1999

10 *Miss Saigon*, Theatre Royal, Drury Lane – opened 20 September 1989 and closed 30 October 1999

FASCINATING FACT

• *The Phantom of the Opera* has grossed £1.8 billion, with total worldwide box office takings of over £3.5 billion ($5.1 billion).

TOP TEN LONGEST-RUNNING SHOWS ON BROADWAY

1   *Phantom of the Opera*, Majestic Theatre – 26 January 1988 to present

2   *Cats*, Winter Garden – 7 October 1982 to 10 September 2000

3   *Les Misérables*, Broadway/Imperial Theatres – 12 March 1987 to 18 May 2003

4   *A Chorus Line*, Schubert Theatre – 25 July 1975 to 28 April 1990

5   *Oh, Calcutta!* – Edison Theatre – 24 September 1976 to 6 August 1989

6   *Chicago* (1996 revival) – Richard Rodgers/Schubert/Ambassador Theatres – 14 November 1996 to present

7   *Beauty and the Beast*, Palace/Lunt-Fontane Theatres – 18 April 1994 to 29 July 2007

8   *The Lion King*, New Amsterdam Theatre – 13 November 1997 to present

9   *Rent*, Nederlander Theatre – 29 April 1996 to 7 September 2008

10 *Miss Saigon* – Broadway Theatre – 11 April 1991 to 28 January 2001

ACTORS THAT HAVE PLAYED HAMLET

YEAR	ACTOR	PLACE PERFORMED
1937	Laurence Olivier	Old Vic
1948	Paul Scofield	Royal Shakespeare Company
1958	Michael Redgrave	Royal Shakespeare Company
1961	Ian Bannen	Royal Shakespeare Company
1963	Peter O'Toole	National Theatre
1964	Richard Burton	Broadway
1965	David Warner	Royal Shakespeare Theatre
1975	Ben Kingsley	Royal Shakespeare Company
1977	Derek Jacobi	Royal Shakespeare Company
1980	Jonathan Pryce	Royal Court
1982	Christopher Walken	American Shakespeare Company
1989	Mark Rylance	Royal Shakespeare Company
1993	Kenneth Branagh	Royal Shakespeare Company
1995	Ralph Fiennes	Broadway
2001–2	Samuel West	Royal Shakespeare Company
2004	Ben Wishaw	Old Vic
2004	Toby Stephens	Royal Shakespeare Company
2008–9	David Tennant	Royal Shakespeare Company
2009	Jude Law	Donmar Warehouse

TEN YEARS OF OLIVIER AWARD WINNERS

YEAR	BEST ACTRESS	BEST ACTOR
2001	Julie Walters *(All My Sons)*	Conleth Hill *(Stones in His Pockets)*
2002	Lindsay Duncan *(Private Lives)*	Roger Allam *(Privates on Parade)*
2003	Clare Higgins *(Vincent in Brixton)*	Simon Russell Beale *(Uncle Vanya)*
2004	Eileen Atkins *(Honour)*	Matthew Kelly *(Of Mice and Men)*
2005	Clare Higgins *(Hecuba)*	Richard Griffiths *(The History Boys)*
2006	Eve Best *(Hedda Gabler)*	Brian Dennehy *(Death of a Salesman)*
2007	Tamsin Greig *(Much Ado About Nothing)*	Rufus Sewell *(Rock 'n' Roll)*
2008	Kristin Scott Thomas *(The Seagull)*	Chiwetel Ejiofor *(Othello)*
2009	Margaret Tyzack *(The Chalk Garden)*	Derek Jacobi *(Twelfth Night)*
2010	Rachel Weisz *(A Streetcar Named Desire)*	Mark Rylance *(Jerusalem)*

TOP TEN MOST OLIVIER AWARD WINS

	NAME	PROFESSION	NO. OF WINS
1	Judi Dench	actress	7
2	William Dudley	designer	7
3	Ian McKellen	actor	6
4	Alan Bennett	actor/writer	6
5	Richard Eyre	director	6
6	Stephen Sondheim	composer	6
7	Matthew Bourne	choreographer/director	5
8	Declan Donnellan	director	5
9	Mark Henderson	lighting designer	5
10	Mark Thompson	designer	5

FIVE YEARS OF TONY AWARD WINNERS

YEAR	ACTOR IN A PLAY	ACTRESS IN A PLAY	ACTOR IN A MUSICAL	ACTRESS IN A MUSICAL
2006	Richard Griffiths *(The History Boys)*	Cynthia Nixon *(Rabbit Hole)*	John Lloyd Young *(Jersey Boys)*	LaChanze *(The Color Purple)*
2007	Frank Langella *(Frost/Nixon)*	Julie White *(The Little Dog Laughed)*	David Hyde Pierce *(Curtains)*	Christine Ebersole *(Grey Gardens)*
2008	Mark Rylance *(Boeing-Boeing)*	Deanna Dunagan *(August Osage County)*	Paulo Szot *(South Pacific)*	Patti LuPone *(Gypsy)*
2009	Geoffrey Rush *(Exit the King)*	Marcia Gay Harden *(God of Carnage)*	David Alvarez, Trent Kowalik and Kiril Kulish *(Billy Elliot)*	Alice Ripley *(Next to Normal)*
2010	Denzel Washington *(Fences)*	Viola Davis *(Fences)*	Douglas Hodge *(La Cage aux Folles)*	Catherine Zeta-Jones *(A Little Night Music)*

FASCINATING FACTS

- The earliest documented performance of *Hamlet* took place on board a ship called *The Dragon*, as it lay anchored off the coast of Sierra Leone in 1607. It was staged by the crew to entertain a visiting dignitary.

- Each Olivier Award is a solid bronze statuette weighing 1.6 kg. It depicts the young Olivier as *Henry V* at The Old Vic in 1937 and was commissioned by The Society of London Theatre from the sculptor Harry Franchetti.

- David Suchet has been nominated no less than six times but has never won an Olivier Award.

- The Tony Award is actually named after a woman. 'Toni' was the nickname for Denver actress Antoinette Perry who later turned successfully to producing and directing.

- Dolores Gray performed the shortest-lived Tony Award-winning role. She won a Tony Award for her performance in *Carnival in Flanders* (1953), a musical that ran only six performances.

# ORIGINS OF THEATRE

Western theatre originated in Ancient Greece. It came out of a state festival in Athens in honour of the god Dionysus. The Athenian city-state exported the festival throughout the Greek Empire to promote a common identity. The basic structure of the Greek theatre can be recognised in our theatres today.

Orchestra – The orchestra (dancing space) was normally circular. It was a level space where the chorus would dance, sing and interact with the actors who were on the stage near the skene. The earliest orchestras were simply made of packed earth but in the Classical period some orchestras began to be paved with marble and other materials. In the centre of the orchestra there was often a thymele (altar).

Theatron – The theatron (viewing-place) is where the spectators sat. The theatron was usually part of a hillside overlooking the orchestra, and often wrapped around a large portion of the orchestra. Spectators in 5 BC probably sat on cushions or boards but by the 4 BC the theatron of many Greek theatres had marble seats.

Skene – The skene (tent) was the building directly behind the stage. The skene was at the back of the stage and was usually decorated as a palace, temple or other building, depending on the needs of the play. It had at least one set of doors, and actors could make entrances and exits through them. There was also access to the roof of the skene from behind, so that actors playing gods and other heavenly characters could appear on the roof.

SHAKESPEARE'S PLAYS

TRAGEDIES

Antony and Cleopatra
Coriolanus
Hamlet, Prince of Denmark
Julius Caesar
King Lear
Macbeth
Othello, Moor of Venice
Romeo and Juliet
Timon of Athens
Titus Andronicus

COMEDIES

All's Well That Ends Well
As You Like It
The Comedy of Errors
Cymbeline
Love's Labour's Lost
Measure for Measure
The Merry Wives of Windsor
The Merchant of Venice
A Midsummer Night's Dream
Much Ado About Nothing
Pericles, Prince of Tyre
The Taming of the Shrew
The Tempest
Troilus and Cressida
Twelfth Night
Two Gentlemen of Verona
The Winter's Tale

HISTORIES

King John
King Richard II
King Henry IV, Part One
King Henry IV, Part Two
King Henry V
King Henry VI, Part One
King Henry VI, Part Two
King Henry VI, Part Three
King Richard III
King Henry VIII

THE SCOTTISH PLAY

To say the name of Shakespeare's *Macbeth* is considered very bad luck among actors. It is said that there is a history of catastrophes, bad luck, and unexplained incidents when the play is performed, and some actors consider it unlucky to refer to the play by name. They call *Macbeth*, 'The Scottish Play'. As to how this superstition arose is subject to debate. It is said that the play, with its witches, spells and incantations, was nervously performed by Shakespeare's actors, and that the fear that the play was cursed was confirmed when an actor by the name of Hal Berridge died while playing Lady Macbeth in 1606. Some argue that the superstition was an invention of a later generation of actors.

There is however much evidence to support an actor's phobia:

- A dispute between actors and an unappreciative audience member in 1721 turned into a riot with the militia and the theatre burned down.

- In 1849, another riot in New York during a production led to 23 deaths and hundreds being injured.

- In the early 1930s, Dame Lillian Boylis took on the role of Lady Macbeth only to die in the dress rehearsal.

- In 1947 Harold Norman, as Macbeth, was fatally stabbed in the sword fight that ends the play.

- Productions in London's West End in the last 70 years are studded with car crashes, bad theatre-related accidents, sudden deaths and suicide. So perhaps if you do say 'Macbeth', it is best to pay homage to the tradition and leave the room, spin round three times, spit, knock thee times and ask to be allowed back in!

COMMON SHAKESPEARE QUOTES AND THEIR ORIGINS

'I am a man more sinned against than sinning'
'Close pent-up guilts/Rive your concealing continents, and cry/These dreadful summoners grace. I am a man/More sinned against than sinning'
King Lear 3.2.59

'You've hoist yourself on your own petar'
'For 'tis the sport to have the engineer/Hoist with his own petar...'*
Hamlet 3.4.206

*To cause the engineer to be blown up by his own bomb; that is, to cause a person to be destroyed by his own deeds. The word 'petar' is obsolete and is synonymous with 'petard', which is defined to be a pasteboard bomb used in fireworks.

'Love is blind...'
'But love is blind, and lovers cannot see/The pretty follies that themselves commit'
The Merchant of Venice 2.6.38–39

TEN OF THE WORLD'S BEST OPERA HOUSES

1   Metropolitan Opera House, New York, USA

2   Sydney Opera House, Sydney, Australia

3   Royal Opera House, London, England

4   Paris Opéra, Paris, France

5   Teatro alla Scala (La Scala), Milan, Italy

6   Teatro La Fenice, Venice, Italy

7   Mariinsky Theatre, St Petersburg, Russia

8   Teatro Real, Madrid, Spain

9   Canolfan Mileniwm Cymru (Wales Millenium Centre), Cardiff, Wales

10 Wiener Staatsoper, Vienna, Austria

TRAVEL

TOP TEN WORLD'S FASTEST AIRCRAFT

	AIRCRAFT	SPEED
1	Space Shuttle	17,500 mph (28,164 km/h)
2	X-43A	7,500 mph (12,070 km/h)
3	X-15	4,510 mph (7,258 km/h)
4	SR-71 Blackbird	2,200 mph (3,540 km/h)
5	MiG-25R Fox bat-B	2,000 mph (3,219 km/h)
6	X-2	1,900 mph (3,058 km/h)
7	XB-70 Valkyrie	1,890 mph (3,042 km/h)
8	F-15 Eagle	1,875 mph (3,017 km/h)
9	MiG-31 Foxhound	1,750 mph (2,816 km/h)
10	F-111 Aardvark	1,650 mph (2,655 km/h)

TOP TEN WORLD'S LARGEST AEROPLANES

	AEROPLANE	WINGSPAN
1	Spruce Goose	97.6 m (320.1 ft)
2	AN-225	88.7 m (291.1 ft)
3	A380	79.8 m (261.7 ft)
4	AN-214	73.3 m (240.5 ft)
5	B-36 Peacemaker	70.1 m (230.1 ft)
6	C-5 Lockheed Galaxy	67.9 m (222.8 ft)
7	Boeing 747	64.4 m (211.4 ft)
8	ANT-20 Tupolev	63.0 m (206.7 ft)
9	Mars Martin	61.7 m (202.5 ft)
10	Boeing 777	60.9 m (199.9 ft)

TOP TEN WORLD'S BUSIEST AIRPORTS*

	AIRPORT	PLACE	NO. OF PASSENGERS PER MONTH
1	Hartsfield-Jackson Atlanta International Airport	Georgia, USA	20,181,931
2	O'Hare International Airport	Chicago, USA	15,346,475
3	London Heathrow Airport	London, UK	15,268,609
4	Tokyo International Airport	Tokyo, Japan	15,180,894
5	Beijing Capital International Airport	Beijing, China	15,153,600
6	Dallas-Fort Worth International Airport	Texas, USA	12,833,031
7	Los Angeles International Airport	California, USA	12,630,858
8	Paris-Charles de Gaulle Airport	Paris, France	12,447,664
9	Denver International Airport	Colorado, USA	11,495,033
10	Hong Kong International Airport	Chek Lap Kok, Hong Kong	11,098,500

* Figures indicate total number of passengers, as of January 2010.

TOP TEN BUSIEST
UK AIRPORTS*

1	London Heathrow	66,036,957
2	London Gatwick	32,392,520
3	London Stansted	19,957,077
4	Manchester	18,724,889
5	London Luton	9,120,546
6	Birmingham	9,102,899
7	Edinburgh	9,049,355
8	Glasgow International	7,225,021
9	Bristol	5,642,921
10	Liverpool	4,884,494

* Figures indicate total number of passengers, as of 2009.

TOP TEN WORLD'S
FASTEST CARS

1   SSC Ultimate Aero – 0-60 mph in 2.7 sec., max. speed: 257 mph

2   Bugatti Veyron – 0-60 mph in 2.5 sec., max. speed: 253 mph

3   Saleen S7 Twin-Turbo – 0-60 mph in 3.2 sec., max. speed: 248 mph

4   Koenigsegg CCX – 0-60 mph in 3.2 sec., max. speed: 245 mph

5   McLaren F1 – 0-60 mph in 3.2 sec., max. speed: 240 mph

6   Ferrari Enzo – 0-60 mph in 3.4 sec., max. speed: 217 mph

7   Jaguar XJ220 – 0-60 mph in 3.8 sec., max. speed: 217 mph

8   Pagani Zonda F – 0-60 mph in 3.5 sec., max. speed: 215 mph

9   Lamborghini Murcielago LP640 – 0-60 mph in 3.3 sec., max. speed: 211 mph

10   Porsche Carrera GT – 0-60 mph in 3.9 sec., max. speed: 205 mph

TOP TEN WORLD'S MOST EXPENSIVE CARS

1	Bugatti Veyron	£1,107,040 ($1,700,000)
2	Lamborghini Reventon	£1,041,920 ($1,600,000)
3	McLaren F1	£631,664 ($970,000)
4	Ferrari Enzo	£436,304 ($670,000)
5	Pagani Zonda C12 F	£434,559 ($667,321)
6	SSC Ultimate Aero	£426,145 ($654,400)
7	Saleen S7 Twin Turbo	£361,416 ($555,000)
8	Koenigsegg CCX	£355,273 ($545,568)
9	Mercedes Benz SLR McLaren Roadster	£322,344 ($495,000)
10	Porsche Carrera GT	£286,528 ($440,000)

TOP TEN BIGGEST CAR MANUFACTURING COUNTRIES

	COUNTRY	NO. OF UNITS MANUFACTURED IN 2009
1	China	10,383,831
2	Japan	6,862,161
3	Germany	4,964,523
4	South Korea	3,158,417
5	Brazil	2,576,628
6	USA	2,249,061
7	India	2,166,238
8	France	1,821,734
9	Spain	1,812,688
10	UK	999,460

NUMBER OF CARS PRODUCED GLOBALLY OVER THE LAST DECADE

YEAR	UNITS PRODUCED	YEAR	UNITS PRODUCED
2000	41,215,653	2005	46,862,978
2001	39,825,888	2006	49,886,549
2002	41,358,394	2007	54,920,317
2003	41,968,666	2008	52,940,559
2004	44,554,268	2009	51,971,328

TOP TEN COUNTRIES WITH THE DEADLIEST ROADS

	COUNTRY	ROAD TRAFFIC DEATHS PER 100,000 OF THE POPULATION
1	Eritrea	48.4
2	Egypt	41.6
3	Libya	40.5
4	Afghanistan	39
5	Iraq	38.1
6	Angola	37.7
7	Niger	37.7
8	United Arab Emirates	37.1
9	The Gambia	36.6
10	Iran	35.8

TOP TEN WORLD'S
BUSIEST SEA PORTS*

1	Singapore	25.8
2	Shanghai, China	25
3	Hong Kong, China	21
4	Shenzhen, China	18
5	Busan, South Korea	12
6	Guangzhou, China	11.1
7	Dubai, UAE	11.1
8	Ningbo, China	10.5
9	Qingdao, China	10.2
10	Rotterdam, Netherlands	10

* Figures indicate how many TEUs (20-foot equivalent units) in their millions were handled in 2009.

TEN OF THE MOST FAMOUS SHIPS THROUGHOUT HISTORY

1. **Titanic** – SS *Titanic* on her maiden voyage struck an iceberg in the North Atlantic and sank with the loss of 1,513 lives on 15 April 1912. She was at the time the world's largest passenger liner and considered unsinkable.

2. HMS **Victory** – Nelson's flagship. Nelson died from a bullet wound on her deck in the Battle of Trafalgar 21 October 2005.

3. **Mayflower** – Ship that transported the pilgrims from Plymouth, England, to Plymouth Colony, Massachusetts, USA in 1620.

4. **Endeavour** – Ship in which Captain James Cook claimed Australia for Britain (1768–71).

5. HMS **Bounty** – The *Bounty* was involved in the most famous mutiny in naval history in 1789. Captain William Bligh and 18 of his crew were set adrift in the Pacific but they survived and safely reached Timor. The mutineers, led by Fletcher Christian, settled on Pitcairn Island where their ancestors still live today.

6. **Mary Rose** – Henry VIII's greatest warship, which sank off Southsea in 1545. It was recovered in 1982 and her remains are on display at Portsmouth.

7. **Marie Celeste** – A USA brigantine found abandoned in the Atlantic in 1872 with absolutely no crew. It was a great mystery as the cargo was intact and the saloon cabin laid for tea.

8. HMS **Beagle** – Carried a young Charles Darwin on its five-year voyage of South America and its islands, which led to the publication of *The Origin of Species*, in 1859.

9. **Niña, Pinta and Santa Maria** – The fleet sailed by Christopher Columbus to the West Indies, the discovery of which opened up the New World in 1492.

10. **Rainbow Warrior** – The international protest ship belonging to the environmental action group, Greenpeace, was badly damaged by two explosions while moored in New Zealand in July 1985.

- Portholes are traditionally round because the constant up and down motion of a ship places a lot of strain and stress on a ship's outer covering. If portholes were designed at angles, the stress would tend to concentrate at those points and crack the outer covering. With portholes being round, this stress is evenly distributed around the holes, making it less likely for these cracks to occur.

THE SHIPPING FORECAST

The shipping forecast is regularly broadcast for the sea areas around the British Isles. From the north of Scotland clockwise, these are the areas:

South-East Iceland	Dover
Faeroes	Wight
Fair Isle	Portland
Viking	Plymouth
North Utsire	Biscay
South Utsire	Finisterre
Cromarty	Sole
Forties	Lundy
Forth	Irish Sea
Dogger	Fastnet
Tyne	Shannon
Humber	Rockall
Fisher	Malin
German Bight	Hebrides
Thames	Bailey

TOP FIVE FASTEST TRAINS IN THE WORLD

	NAME	COUNTRY	MAX. SPEED
1	*JR Maglev*	Japan	361 mph (581 km/h)
2	*TGV*	France	357.2 mph (574.8 km/h)
3	*Shanghai Maglev*	China	268 mph (431 km/h)
4	*CRH* (China Railway High-speed)	China	245 mph (394.3 km/h)
5	*AVE* (Alta Velocidad Española)	Spain	186 mph (300 km/h)

FASCINATING FACT

- The *JR Maglev* in Japan set the world speed record for a manned, railed vehicle when it hit 361 mph on 2 December 2003.

TEN OF THE MOST FAMOUS
TRAINS THROUGH HISTORY

1   *Orient Express* – The two city names most intimately associated
    with the *Orient Express* are Paris and Istanbul, whereas the
    modern regular scheduled train that bears the name now
    does not serve either. The current *Orient Express* runs from
    Strasbourg to Vienna leaving Strasbourg at 10.20 p.m. daily.

2   *Flying Scotsman* – This passenger train has run between London
    and Edinburgh since 1862. It is currently operated by GNER.

3   **Trans-Siberian Railway** – This is a network of railways
    connecting Moscow and European Russia with the Russian Far
    East provinces, Mongolia, China and the Sea of Japan. It was
    built between 1891 and 1916, and is 5,772 miles (9,288 km)
    long. It spans eight time zones and takes about seven days to
    complete its journey.

4   **Burma Railway** – Also known as the 'Death Railway' is a 258
    m (415 km) railway between Bangkok, Thailand and Rangoon,
    Myanmar (Burma), built by the Empire of Japan during World
    War Two to support its forces in the Burma campaign. Forced
    labour was used in its construction and over 100,000 Asian
    labourers and 16,000 Allied POWs died as a direct result of the
    project.

5   *Glacier Express* – Running from Zermatt to St Moritz in
    Switzerland, this train is not an express in the 'high-speed'
    sense of the term, but rather that it provides a one-seat ride
    from end to end (even though the train travels over several
    different railroad lines). It is a 7½-hour railway journey across
    291 bridges, through 91 tunnels and across the Oberalp Pass at
    2,033 m in altitude.

6   *Blue Train* – This train travels a 1,000-mile (1,600-km) journey
    between Pretoria and Cape Town in South Africa. It is one of the
    most luxurious train journeys in the world.

7   *20th Century Limited* – An express passenger train operated by
    the New York Central Railroad from 1902 to 1967, during which
    time it became the 'Most Famous Train in the World'. Known for
    its speed as well as for its style, passengers walked to and from
    the train on a plush, crimson carpet, which was rolled out at
    station stops, thus the 'red carpet treatment' was born.

8   *Ghan* - This is the 48-hour, 2,979 km passenger train which travels from Adelaide, through Alice Springs to Darwin. The service's name is an abbreviated version of its previous nickname 'The Afghan Express', which comes from the Afghan camel trains that trekked the same route before the advent of the railway.

9   *Rheingold Express* – This legendary train traversed between Hoek van Holland near Rotterdam and Basel, Switzerland, a distance of 662 km. Its operation ended in 1987 after 59 years and 15 days.

10   *Brighton Belle* – This Pullman service ran from 1934 between Victoria Station, London to Brighton on the Sussex coast until its withdrawal from service on 20 April 1972.

FASCINATING FACT

- The London Underground was the world's first underground railway when it opened on 10 January 1863. It is also the world's longest underground with 251 miles of track.

TOP FIVE WORLD'S FASTEST STREET-LEGAL BIKES

	NAME	MAX. SPEED
1	Ducati Desmosedici RR	199 mph (320 km/h)
2	MV Agusta F4 1100 cc	196 mph (315 km/h)
3	MV Agusta F4 1000 MT Tamburini	191 mph (307 km/h)
4	Kawasaki ZX-12R Ninja	189 mph (305 km/h)
5	Suzuki GSX 1300 R Hayabusa	186 mph (300 km/h)

FASCINATING FACTS

- The longest motorbike ride through a tunnel of fire was completed in January 2008 in Los Angeles at a record 60.96 m (200 ft).

- The tallest rideable motorbike was made in the USA, and is 3.429 m (11 ft 3 in.) tall, and has an 8.2 litre engine.

- The record for the longest backwards motorcycle ride is 93.21 miles (150 km) and was achieved in Binzhou City, China, on October 4 2006.

TOP TEN WORLD'S MOST POPULAR TOURIST DESTINATIONS

	COUNTRY	INTERNATIONAL TOURIST ARRIVALS IN 2009
1	France	74.2 million
2	USA	54.9 million
3	Spain	52.2 million
4	China	50.9 million
5	Italy	43.2 million
6	UK	28 million
7	Turkey	25.5 million
8	Germany	24.2 million
9	Malaysia	23.6 million
10	Mexico	21.5 million

FASCINATING FACTS

- The fastest elevator in the world resides in the Taipei 101 Tower in Taiwan, reaching a top speed of 37 mph.

TOP TEN WORLD'S LARGEST HOTELS

1 **First World Hotel**, Malaysia: 6,000 rooms. Best Feature: an indoor theme park.

2 **MGM Grand,** Las Vegas, USA: 5,044 rooms. Best Feature: a 1000 ft-long pool.

3 **Luxor,** Las Vegas, USA: 4,408 rooms. Best Feature: the hotel is in the shape of a pyramid, and features a replica of the tomb of Tutankhamen.

4 **Ambassador City Jomtien Hotel**, Thailand: 4,239 rooms. Best Feature: situated on a coastline known for its windsailing and surfing opportunities.

5 **Hilton Hawaiian Village Beach**, Honolulu, USA: 3,386 rooms. Best Feature: the hotel has a wildlife habitat, fireworks shows and submarine rides.

6 **Palazzo**, Las Vegas, USA: 3,066 rooms. Best Feature: it is styled like a plush Italian villa, with Roman baths.

7 **Venetian Macao**, China: 3,000 rooms. Best Feature: many activities on offer, including gondola rides.

8 **Paris**, Las Vegas, USA: 2,916 rooms. Best Feature: a 164.6 m (541 ft) replica of the Eiffel Tower at the front of the hotel.

9 **Gaylord Opryland**, Tennessee, USA: 2,881 rooms. Best Feature: beautiful indoor gardens featuring a river.

10 **Pop Century Resort (Walt Disney World)**, Florida, USA: 2,880 rooms. Best Feature: every area of the hotel is dedicated to the decor of each decade from the 1950s to the 1990s.

TOP TEN WORLD'S MOST VISITED CITIES

1	Paris	France
2	London	United Kingdom
3	Bangkok	Thailand
4	Singapore	Singapore
5	Kuala Lumpur	Malaysia
6	New York City	USA
7	Dubai	UAE
8	Istanbul	Turkey
9	Hong Kong	Hong Kong
10	Shanghai	China

TOP TEN WORLD'S MOST VISITED TOURIST ATTRACTIONS*

	PLACE	COUNTRY	NUMBER OF VISITORS IN 2007
1	Times Square	NYC, USA	35 million
2	National Mall and Memorial Parks	Washington DC, USA	25 million
3	Disney World's Magic Kingdom	Florida, USA	16.6 million
4	Trafalgar Square	London, England	15 million
5	Disneyland Park	California, USA	14.7 million
6	Niagra Falls	Ontario, Canada	14 million
7	Golden Gate National Recreation Area	San Francisco, USA	13 million
8	Tokyo Disneyland/ DisneySea	Japan	12.9 million
9	Notre Dame de Paris	France	12 million
10	Disneyland Paris	France	10.6 million

* Figures represent number of visitors in 2007.

TOP TEN WORLD'S MOST VISITED MUSEUMS

MUSEUM	PLACE	COUNTRY	NUMBER OF VISITORS PER YEAR
1 Musée du Louvre	Paris	France	8,500,000
2 British Museum	London	UK	5,569,981
3 Metropolitan Museum of Art	New York City	USA	4,891,450
4 National Gallery	London	UK	4,780,030
5 Tate Modern	London	UK	4,747,537
6 National Gallery of Art	Washington DC	USA	4,605,606
7 Centre Georges Pompidou	Paris	France	3,530,000
8 Musée d'Orsay	Paris	France	3,022,012
9 Museo del Prado	Madrid	Spain	2,763,094
10 National Museum of Korea	Seoul	South Korea	2,730,204